Trade Like
a Shark

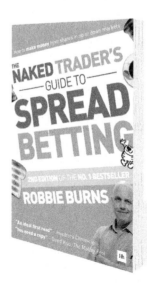

Trade Like a Shark

How to eat and not get eaten
in the stock market

Robbie Burns

Every owner of a physical copy of this edition of

TRADE LIKE
A SHARK

can download the eBook for free direct from us at Harriman House, in a DRM-free format that can be read on any eReader, tablet or smartphone.

Simply head to:

EBOOKS.HARRIMAN-HOUSE.COM/ TRADELIKEASHARK

to get your copy now.

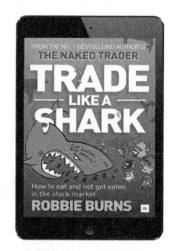

HARRIMAN HOUSE LTD
18 College Street
Petersfield
Hampshire
GU31 4AD
GREAT BRITAIN

Tel: +44 (0)1730 233870
Email: enquiries@harriman-house.com
Website: www.harriman-house.com

First published in Great Britain in 2016.

Paperback ISBN: 978-0-85719-542-5
eBook ISBN: 978-0-85719-543-2

British Library Cataloguing in Publication Data
A CIP catalogue record for this book can be obtained from the British Library.

Price chart images copyright © ShareScope.
Cartoons copyright © Pete Dredge 2014, 2016.
Toast pieces copyright © iStockphoto.
Shark silhouettes © Sunny Art Shop.

Set in Plantin and Clarendon.

Contents

About the Author

Robbie Burns has been a full-time trader since 2001 when he quit his day job for sitting in his pants in his living room with a laptop.

He wrote the *Sunday Times* 'My DIY Pension' column and now writes monthly columns for ADVFN.com and Master Investor. He also writes a diary and lists all his new trades at his website: **www.nakedtrader.co.uk**

He has won three awards: Best Looking Bald Trader in his road— well, OK, *two* awards: Best Educational Finance Provider 2015 and Best Financial Blogger 2016 at the International Finance Awards. He is envious that his trophies are dwarfed on the mantelpiece by the 15 football trophies won by his son.

He works very hard all day from home. He certainly doesn't spend most days lazing around watching *Game of Thrones* and eating biscuits. He works very, very hard and prides himself on being an unemotional trader.

He's become one of the country's 250-odd ISA millionaires (building more than £1 million tax-free from an average of around only £10,000 of funds per year). He's also made substantial tax-free sums from spread betting and owns two £1m-plus London properties debt-free.

Robbie has written four editions of his bestseller, *The Naked Trader*, two editions of *The Naked Trader's Guide to Spread Betting* and has a debut novel on the way.

Robbie works properly for six days a year when he hosts seminars for traders and investors, teaching his methods live from the markets. He refuses to take part in investor days, speeches, talks, etc. as he would miss *Deal or No Deal*.

Robbie is married, with one son aged 11. He enjoys terrible dance music, awful TV, and eats too many Twix bars and too much toast and jam. His dentist drives a Maserati.

Preface

My qualifications

What are my qualifications for writing a book on psychology? Absolutely none whatsoever. I didn't even go to university. But I do have 16 years' experience trading shares in all kinds of market conditions. And I have met thousands of traders and investors. Hundreds have sent me stories of their experiences in the markets over the years. I have discussed trading psychology with groups of traders of every background and skill level.

It would be hard for this not to give me a strong idea of what works and what doesn't. I should also say that my 16 years in the markets have been successful ones. Boasting, as we will see later in the book, is not a good idea for traders, so I am technically begging for a 12-pack of eggs on my face by mentioning that fact. Nevertheless, because I don't want you to think that I'm just blathering on about something I've read a lot of Wikipedia articles about, you should know that I am one of only around 250

'ISA millionaires' in the UK. That's someone who has managed to turn their ISA contributions (around £10,000 a year when you average it out) into more than £1 million simply through buying and selling shares.

It wasn't easy. But if I could do it, well, there's really no reason you can't – as my wife will be the first to tell you.

Many books on trading psychology are written by highly qualified people who have studied the subject, and that's great – but I think they're missing the biggest qualification of all: experience. And, above all, experience of getting it right. (Not that I haven't got it wrong at times...)

Who this book is for

This book is for anyone currently trading or investing – from beginner to experienced – as well as anyone thinking about taking it up. No particular experience of trading is needed to be able to read this book. Indeed, some of you might find it fun to read about people who screwed up (you sadistic bastards).

If you are a beginner or improver, stuff about how to trade, do research, market timing and all the tools you need to trade are in my other book, *The Naked Trader*.

In that book and in my guide to spread betting I cover everything from what it means to be a trader or investor, through to how to find shares with potential and detailed strategies on making money from trading them in markets of all kinds.

Thanks for buying any of them. I get about 50p for each one, while Amazon gets... actually, I had better not dwell on how much Amazon gets or I'll be violating a key tenet of being a successful trader (anger doesn't help).

I want this book to be enjoyable, so there is no psychobabble. I don't use long words (I don't know any except 'psychobabble', which I can't spell) or any silly jargon.

As I said, I have no qualifications of any kind – but I can give you access to a wealth of experience built up over years of trading successfully and meeting and chatting with traders and investors of all kinds.

Simplicity itself

The world of trading shares can seem scary. It's no wonder traders get into such a mess. And most really do. Even the very best. The statistics are frightening. The message of this book is that things can – and should – be simple. Simple is the way to win.

Warren Buffett put it well when he said:

"There seems to be some perverse human characteristic that likes to make easy things difficult."

Exactly, Warren! This book is designed to make your trading simple by making sure you don't fill your mind with junk that makes it all the more difficult.

Ben Graham (the father of value investing) said:

"The investor's chief problem – and even his worst enemy – is likely to be himself."

Ben and Warren are so wise. All I ever say is: "Is my tea ready yet?" But Ben's comment is a lot of what this book is about – how you can destroy yourself. But not if you are forewarned and forearmed.

I am going to show you how.

As you might have gathered from the book's cover, I think the simplest way to keep it simple is to trade like a shark.

I want you to stop being nice! You have got to be nasty, businesslike – shark-like.

You have to get those teeth out, bare them and be totally ruthless in cutting losing positions and running the winning ones. You have to make sure you know more than the fishes and execute all your plans with ruthless efficiency.

So no more Mr Nice Guy. No sitting and hoping on the ocean floor while the shark comes to get you. I am going to teach you to be the shark gobbling the fish!

Robbie

LONDON, 2016

After all, a shark's life *is* pretty straightforward when you think about it. As long as they can avoid being shot by Massachusetts police chiefs, all they have to do is pursue their prey – smaller fishes – and gobble them up. They are ruthless and focused. And successful.

This is a good analogy for the markets. In the markets, the sharks win. They gobble up the money from the fishes. The fishes are all panicked, swimming about, not knowing what to do – the sharks pounce and eat them up.

In market terms, the sharks take their money from the fishes. When someone wins in the market, someone else is on the losing side. The fish.

Most people in the market are fishes. They are swimming about panicking, worried, fearful, greedy – full of different emotions. The sharks are intent on one thing alone: taking the fishes' cash.

I want this book to help you turn from trading like a fish to trading like a shark.

I want this book to be enjoyable, so there is no psychobabble. I don't use long words (I don't know any except 'psychobabble', which I can't spell) or any silly jargon.

As I said, I have no qualifications of any kind – but I can give you access to a wealth of experience built up over years of trading successfully and meeting and chatting with traders and investors of all kinds.

Simplicity itself

The world of trading shares can seem scary. It's no wonder traders get into such a mess. And most really do. Even the very best. The statistics are frightening. The message of this book is that things can – and should – be simple. Simple is the way to win.

Warren Buffett put it well when he said:

> "There seems to be some perverse human characteristic that likes to make easy things difficult."

Exactly, Warren! This book is designed to make your trading simple by making sure you don't fill your mind with junk that makes it all the more difficult.

Ben Graham (the father of value investing) said:

> "The investor's chief problem – and even his worst enemy – is likely to be himself."

Ben and Warren are so wise. All I ever say is: "Is my tea ready yet?" But Ben's comment is a lot of what this book is about – how you can destroy yourself. But not if you are forewarned and forearmed.

I am going to show you how.

As you might have gathered from the book's cover, I think the simplest way to keep it simple is to trade like a shark.

'ISA millionaires' in the UK. That's someone who has managed to turn their ISA contributions (around £10,000 a year when you average it out) into more than £1 million simply through buying and selling shares.

It wasn't easy. But if I could do it, well, there's really no reason you can't – as my wife will be the first to tell you.

Many books on trading psychology are written by highly qualified people who have studied the subject, and that's great – but I think they're missing the biggest qualification of all: experience. And, above all, experience of getting it right. (Not that I haven't got it wrong at times…)

Who this book is for

This book is for anyone currently trading or investing – from beginner to experienced – as well as anyone thinking about taking it up. No particular experience of trading is needed to be able to read this book. Indeed, some of you might find it fun to read about people who screwed up (you sadistic bastards).

If you are a beginner or improver, stuff about how to trade, do research, market timing and all the tools you need to trade are in my other book, *The Naked Trader*.

In that book and in my guide to spread betting I cover everything from what it means to be a trader or investor, through to how to find shares with potential and detailed strategies on making money from trading them in markets of all kinds.

Thanks for buying any of them. I get about 50p for each one, while Amazon gets… actually, I had better not dwell on how much Amazon gets or I'll be violating a key tenet of being a successful trader (anger doesn't help).

Preface

My qualifications

What are my qualifications for writing a book on psychology? Absolutely none whatsoever. I didn't even go to university. But I do have 16 years' experience trading shares in all kinds of market conditions. And I have met thousands of traders and investors. Hundreds have sent me stories of their experiences in the markets over the years. I have discussed trading psychology with groups of traders of every background and skill level.

It would be hard for this not to give me a strong idea of what works and what doesn't. I should also say that my 16 years in the markets have been successful ones. Boasting, as we will see later in the book, is not a good idea for traders, so I am technically begging for a 12-pack of eggs on my face by mentioning that fact. Nevertheless, because I don't want you to think that I'm just blathering on about something I've read a lot of Wikipedia articles about, you should know that I am one of only around 250

INTRODUCTION

The other six seconds

Did you know that roughly 70% of investors lose over time, as do 95% of day traders? When I learned those figures I was surprised. I thought more people would be winners. I'd managed it over a long period of time so I figured maybe at least half would make something.

What was it that made so many people lose?

I found the subject fascinating. My publishers kept egging me on to write something about it. But things got in the way. Every time I thought about starting to write anything there was always something better to do. Hang on, *Deal or No Deal* is starting. Hmmm, I'll do it tomorrow, time for a cup of tea and a Twix.

I realised: I'm just a lazy git. How come I could make money out of the stock market, indeed trade full-time for 16 years, when most others couldn't? Something really strange had to be going on.

I wasn't any better at research, analysis, maths – frankly, in a world war I'd be the first one killed for being useless. I can't change a plug; I have no idea what to do if anything electrical goes wrong. In the last stand against ISIS on Hammersmith Bridge I'll be cowering behind the alpha males with their baseball bats.

It turned out the answer was right in front of me all along.

Over the years I've met thousands of traders and investors at seminars I've held. Before each seminar I send them all questionnaires to find out everything I can about what they need help with in their trading. And I follow the progress of many of them after the seminars. Some turn a corner. Some only get worse. Some do brilliantly and then blow up and try to start again.

What makes some successful and some totally hopeless? Why do some continue to achieve? Why do some do well, then collapse and lose?

Looking over our time together, it became obvious. Even more so when I read back over many of the thousands of email discussions I have had with traders and investors asking for my help, or when I think about what I have learned from talking with high-profile traders and industry 'experts'.

It is all down to psychology. The answer lies in the brain. Apparently we men think about sex every seven seconds. Unfortunately, the other six seconds can be spent doing far less productive things: getting over-excited, panicking, getting greedy, being stubborn, losing it, regretting things. Women are not immune either, though as we'll see in chapter 17 they may have some advantages.

The human mind is a tricky thing.

What the best do

Traders I have met who went on to do well became unemotional about their trading and treated it as a business. Though it could take time to get to that stage, anyone who did it found he or she became a lot more successful. They were determined, kept their brains clear of crap, stuck to their rules and maintained strict discipline. Their trading accounts started showing healthy profits.

The ones that did badly were hopelessly emotional about the whole thing. They spent hours trying to get it right – got caught up in lots of different strategies, confused themselves, took wild gambles. Refused to sell losers.

They lied to themselves and others about their losses. They repeated mistakes time and time again. They got into terrible states. Their brains were filled with jargon, nonsense, platitudes, other people's ideas, fear, greed, Facebook, Twitter…

When I saw how important it was not to let emotions or other clutter interfere with your trading, I got a big picture of Mr Spock printed and put it up at my seminars and said:

"Think like a Vulcan."

As everyone knows, Mr Spock is an alien from the planet Vulcan. Vulcans are totally unemotional, cold and calculating. Every decision they make must be based on cool, hard logic.

Which is exactly what all the best traders do. Business decisions taken logically, captain. I can't imagine Mr Spock is much good in bed but you can't have everything in life.

Mr Spock's impulsive boss, Captain Kirk, would be a lousy trader – though doubtless pretty amazing in bed (probably behind a rock on a strange planet). Why? Because Kirk is emotional. He takes mad decisions on the spur of the moment. He is the anti-Spock. He'd be going in and out of shares at warp factor nine. (I think the ship blows up at warp ten.)

This book is all about how to be Spock-like and not Kirk-like – at least in your trading. There are tons of times in your life when you do not want to be using a Vulcan brain. Life is for living and Spock was pretty darn boring, except for the time he got high after sniffing plants on a strange planet.

But making money the boring way is really the only way to do it. Save the Kirk in you for enjoying what it can bring you later.

Why this book and not another?

I've been meaning to write a book on trading psychology for years. It's something I covered a bit in my earlier books but it's such a crucial issue that it really needs a whole book to do it justice. *The Naked Trader* helps you to become a technically proficient trader – but there is a difference between being a technically proficient trader and consistently making money. This book bridges that gap.

There are some good books on trading psychology already available – my only problem with them is how boring they are. While I like bits of them, other parts bore the pants off me and I stop reading. Or I skim a bit then get bored.

What's the point of good advice if it goes unread?

So I have written this book as one that I would like to read in the hope that others will enjoy it too – and benefit from it in their trading. It won't get bogged down in facts and figures or deep psychology. Those other books have a lot of theory in them but I don't believe many of the authors have spoken with thousands of traders and investors like I have. I feel I can give some insight into the minds of a lot of people who have traded and failed. Throughout I'll be talking about real people and real examples – not just theory.

The book examines all the ways our brains can sabotage our trading, with examples of where real-life traders have gone wrong and what made them losers. Once you have learned from their mistakes I give you some tips on how to transform your cluttered emotional brain into a cool shark-like one.

See if you can recognise your own flaws somewhere along the line. I hope at some point you'll say – "Yes, that's me. That's what I do. That is the part of my brain I have to concentrate on and try to put right."

This book is called *Trade Like a Shark* and that's exactly what you have to do to win: you've got to be cold, ruthless, efficient, unemotional. However, as there are only so many fish puns a person can take and you probably don't want me putting you off your toast by comparing setting up trailing stops to dismembering swimmers, I'll often use other metaphors throughout the book. I'm particularly partial to *Star Trek* and Mr Spock, so one I'll keep coming back to is that idea of being a Vulcan. I do this so many times I might have even called the book *Trade Like Spock* but my publisher didn't want to get sued. Anyway, shark or Spock, it's all very much the same – though I guess Spock never actually ate anyone as far as I can remember.

I have to admit I sometimes struggle keeping my brain shark-like (or Vulcan). Occasionally I will have an attack of the Kirks (or the minnows). It might sound easy keeping to the ideals but it can be quite difficult.

Anyhow, I will do my best to train up that emotional old brain of yours and kick it into shape. Admitting you haven't been trading like a shark is half the battle. We'll work our way through all your failings (and mine). I hope you enjoy it – I promise not to bombard you with psychobabble, drivel or spam mail. After all, I'm not your boss…

And I absolutely swear: I will never ever tell you to 'think outside the box'.

PART I:
The Way of the Shark

It's a Business Not a Hobby!

I'm pretty certain that the main reason I've been able to make a lot of money trading over the years is that I have trained my brain to be more like a character out of 1960s' science fiction.

It sounds weird when you put it like that, but it's true! I think it is the reason I am one of the very few ISA (tax-free) millionaires in the UK thanks to my stock market trading.

I'm not relying on anyone else to do this work for me. I don't read stuff anyone has written about a share I am looking at. I look calmly at the facts and figures. Logically, what are the good points about the share? What are the risks? Where shall I get out if I've got it wrong? And what am I after from the trade?

After all my detective work is done, if I am certain I have more chance of it going up then down, I will make the trade.

I don't understand people who just buy something for no reason other than someone else told them to. Or people who buy an oil company that might not find any. Or who buy an oil company when the oil price is sinking.

One of the main reasons to think of trading with a cold, unemotional brain is that in effect your trading is exactly the same as running a business.

If you are running trading as a true business then each trade you make is like a business purchase. Just as a restaurant buys ingredients to make meals, in effect selling those ingredients on at a higher price to make a profit, we are trying to buy a bit of a company that will increase in value to give us a profit.

Lots of people new to trading think of it as a hobby. It isn't. If you run your trading account as a hobby you'll lose.

"If you're investing for excitement, you are a damn fool."
John Bogle, founder, The Vanguard Group

The best businesses are ruthless

The best businesses, frankly, are run by individuals just as ruthless as sharks. Those at the top of their game – the bosses – are often unemotional and skilled at making difficult decisions that are for the ultimate good of their companies.

So when it comes to firing an employee they will do it unemotionally – or in a bigger company they'll make someone from HR do it. It doesn't mean to say the bosses are bad people, they just have to make a tough decision. And once done, that's it.

Maybe in the evening they tell their partner: "I wish I didn't have to do it." But they still did it. The ultimate goal is to make sure their company is a winner. If they don't cut the jobs, maybe the company will go bust and everyone ends up on the streets.

When I worked at Sky – and later, when I ran my own café – I had to fire people. I didn't like doing it but was firm about it when I did. I even had to fire a woman who was a blackbelt at karate. I made sure I was behind a desk and ready to duck beneath it or make a run down the fire escape in case she tried to karate chop me in the nuts. She took it well, actually. It was a shame to let her go but she had been stealing cash!

If you add them up over the years, I fired quite a few people before ending up as a full-time home trader. Each time it was because it was best for the business. In effect I was cutting a loss. Or potential future loss, as the employee wasn't performing, wasn't right for the job – whatever the reason.

And it is exactly the same with trading. If you are trading you must run it in the same way as you'd run a business.

You have to be ruthless, clear-headed and logical. You have to make tough decisions when you need to and make them quickly. Whatever it takes for your business to succeed.

A shark-like businessman

A shark's mind is clear, logical and if need be ruthless. So was Mr Spock's: if he had to sacrifice one person to save 50, he'd do it without hesitation – even if that person was himself. The needs of the many outweigh the few.

An interesting example of a businessman who reminds me of a shark (or Mr Spock) is someone who, in *The Naked Trader*, I joked would make a great share trader: Alan Sugar. But I'm not really joking!

You might not be the biggest fan of Lord "IwaselllincomputersoffthebackofavanwhenIwoz14" Sugar but in business he definitely knows how to act like a shark.

I'm not saying he's the world's best businessman. What makes him successful isn't never making mistakes – it's the way he has a track record of looking at what has worked and what hasn't and why. He then takes action as soon as possible.

In his show *The Apprentice*, Sir A shows his ruthless streak by firing candidates quickly and easily. Even when it is obvious he likes them personally. Then he tends to say, "With regret, you're fired". This is exactly the same as cutting a losing share without emotion. Maybe next time you cut a share you like, as you press the sell button, say: "With regret, you are sold."

He hasn't always been 100% a shark. The Amstrad E-m@iler (yes, that's how he spelled it) was an epic failure. It was an old-fashioned landline telephone with an LCD screen, keyboard and ridiculous business model, with adverts on-screen and emails that cost as much as one of those dodgy late-night phone lines to check (ahem, so I'm told). Analysis showed that it would add £150 a month to people's phone bills even with low use.

People stampeded not to buy it.

Sugar stuck with the damn things for several years, throwing good money after bad, and then even more money after that.

So even a true shark can have a patchy record – and get better with time. There is hope for us all!

If Lord A was a trader, how would you see his shark-like instincts at work? He would instantly cut losing positions, the same way he would instantly fire someone because he or she wasn't working out.

He wouldn't even worry about it – it's just a small business loss, it happens, that's it. You wouldn't find him sitting on a huge loss these days.

Not taking losses quickly is one of the biggest reasons most traders fail. A share falls, falls some more and the trader feels he is stuck in the losing position instead of just quitting.

Mr Spock would be just as ruthless. Spock and Lord A would either take a quick loss, or set a **stop-loss** with their brokers so that the share is sold unemotionally for them if it falls a set amount.

And logically and unemotionally they would both run their profits as much as they could, allowing good shares to go up to make the big money. They would know the market can get volatile so they would use a **trailing stop**, which goes up with the share price, but keep it far enough away that they don't get kicked out of a trade too early.

They wouldn't get emotionally involved with a share. They've run through some logical research, checked the chart, looked at debt, thought about supply and demand. They don't care what anyone else thinks about the trade. Spock isn't going to ask Captain Kirk whether it's a good idea to buy Barclays. Lord A might ask one of his sidekicks who he should fire but, let's face it, he already knows.

Neither are interested in noise from social media. Nor are they feeling greedy or fearful. I guess this book is really about teaching you how to emulate these would-be amazing traders.

"Those traders who have confidence in their own trades, who trust themselves to do what needs to be done without hesitation, are the ones who become successful. They no longer fear the erratic behaviour of the market. They learn to focus on the information that helps them spot opportunities to make a profit, rather than focusing on the information that reinforces their fears."

Mark Douglas

A bunch of minnows – Traders: Millions By The Minute

So having a shark's view of the markets is really all about the ruthless running of a business, in this case a trading business. Lots of people don't get this at all. They treat it like a lifestyle choice. But sharks don't go swimming for leisure.

The BBC ran a show about new traders called *Traders: Millions By the Minute* (2014). The idea was to follow new and experienced traders and see how they got on. Guess what the new traders all dreamed of. Getting a supercar? A yacht? Getting off with someone half their age now they were rich? No.

They dreamt of six lovely big TV screens. In their office in their house. Mmmm, lovely big screens with charts on them, and Bloomberg and CNBC and oh, lots of lovely charts and tons of information all coming in, just like those traders you see on the telly!

With this kind of attitude it won't be long before instead of watching TV they are living it: bankrupt and trying to find some 'Cash in the Attic'.

Right at the start, those dreams of screens tell me they won't trade like a shark. Screens like that are there to show off to mates or the partner. "Ooh, look at me, the trader." The screens will fire stuff at them all day long, stuff they don't need and stuff that will fill their head and ensure their brain gets so... stuffed... they won't be able to think straight.

They don't need six screens. One will do (that's all I have). We'll talk a lot in this book about how to cut down on stuff that isn't necessary.

This show really is mandatory viewing for traders, particularly because of two bitter-sweet stories it tells. You can tell the subjects of these stories are both kind-hearted, lovable people – but neither had the trading psychology needed to make a go of it.

Trading kittens for losses

The first story was about a lovely mum of small kids, Jane. She'd do anything for them and was really keen to make more money – she had to work as a nurse at weekends to help make ends meet.

She had met a mum on the school run one morning and that mum was driving a rather swish new car. School-run mum confided in her that she had been trading and winning, hence the new car.

Jane immediately coveted school-run mum's new car and pondered whether she could also make money trading. The only thing was: she didn't have any spare money to trade with. She came up with a plan to breed some fancy pedigree kittens that she could flog and in the meantime decided to try virtual trading.

She opened a spread betting account with £300,000 of pretend cash and she couldn't believe how well she was soon doing. After nine months she had built up tons of pretend money, more than a million quid.

She said: "My virtual account is worth £1.5 million. I can't believe how easy it is to make money."

Heaps of cash were already appearing before her eyes and she could see the end of having to be a nurse at weekends. She did find the virtual account a bit stressful, though. And the whole thing a little confusing. Her method was:

"Looking at charts and guessing which way it is going to go."

She told the reporter at her house: "I might just put another one on now as I haven't got a trade open at the moment."

She put a trade on a currency and hoped it would fall. It shot up right away. "Best not to watch – it is too stressful" she said, closing the laptop.

She managed to flog off the posh pussies and had £6,000 to open a real spread betting account. She decided to trade currencies. The cameras followed her first week. She made £99 on her first day, £105 on her second. Then calamity. She lost £350 on day three.

"I risked too much," she said. "My mistake was putting on a £30 trade instead of a £3 one. It's a horrible start and has made me feel sick. I must be careful not to make any more mistakes."

She didn't seem to have much more of an idea of what would make her money than when she was trading with fake money.

"I look at the four-hour chart then the five-minute chart," she said uncertainly. "I feel anxious and reckless and excited when going into profit. I may have lost my bottle … I will be more confident.

"The children want to borrow my iPad to watch *Frozen* while I am trying to trade which can be tricky. I bet City boys don't have to deal with that … Hang on, look, I made £50 today [day four]. I like that. Much nicer to sit at home than go out nursing."

At the end of the show, text flashed up telling the viewer what happened next. After two weeks of trades Jane had £3,856 left. She had blown £2,144 of her £6,000 start-up money.

I am pretty confident that Jane eventually ended up losing the lot. Indeed, with spread betting she might have done something worse. Spread betting lets you borrow huge sums of money with relatively little in your account. Unlike ordinary trading with a broker, it is perfectly possibly to not only lose all your money – but thousands of pounds of someone else's too. I only hope she stopped before she blew more than the £6,000 she had started with.

I don't think Jane was a suitable trading candidate. Almost everything she said was a clue as to what she was doing wrong.

She had no plan. There was no research or analysis of any sort. She didn't look at any news or seem to have any grasp of why a currency would move up or down. She had no idea of how much she was prepared to lose on a trade. She didn't think about timescale. She made trades for the sake of it. It was just press and hope.

After that, she was at the mercy of her emotions. As we will see in part II, they can be deadly for trading success even if you *have* got a plan in place because it takes discipline to overcome them. Without a plan and without discipline, her trading was doomed. She felt "anxious, reckless and excited". Those three words would never describe someone trading like a shark. They describe someone capable of losing a lot of money.

"The big ones take the psychology out of the game. Have a game plan, and stick to it."

Tim Erbe

The one good thing about her trading was that her mind didn't seem to be full of stuff from social media. Unfortunately, it was full of more than enough emotions to compensate.

She had been seduced by the tale of the school-run mum and her trading profits. She hadn't followed that up with Spock-like questioning. She should have quizzed that mum and asked her about all the methods that had made her money.

Most likely, the school-run mum was making stuff up to impress Jane.

Seven years into debt

Another chap filmed as part of this BBC show said he simply "loved trading". Yet after seven years – *seven years* – of trading he had not made any profit at all!

Unlike Jane he said he had a good understanding and good trading plan. Like Jane he was trying to trade currencies.

In his first week of trading he had lost £2,000. After eventually managing to break-even, he decided to contain any losses by reducing the amount he traded. He told the cameras: "In the last two months I have made no progress. I am up by a tenner. My brain is telling me to do something and that seems to work: the trades don't fail but I don't get enough of them."

Having to close out a losing trade is hard and he struggled to manage it.

At a poker night he arranged, his sister Rene wondered why he gave up his previous living as an antiques dealer.

"You could earn money very quickly so you were successful," she said.

He replied: "Although I could make money I felt empty inside and I could see no purpose to my life. Trading gives me emotions antiques never could."

"But you never made any money trading in seven years."

"My self-esteem isn't as good as it should be but I have found a career that is worthy of me and what I want to do."

His sister pressed: "But financially you are not making the money you need."

"But I am happy in what I do even if my lifestyle has gone downhill."

His sister admitted defeat:

"I admire your passion even though you know if you went back to antiques you would make a lot of money. You are either crazy or admirable."

(She obviously thinks he is crazy.)

In the end he said: "I am a trader and that's what I want to be."

No trader in his right mind would spend seven years doing something with the object to make money and then continue when no money is made.

I wonder about the low self-esteem. That must be a hindrance. I don't know how that could be changed. Possibly if you have low self-esteem trading won't be for you because you do not see yourself as worthy of being a winner.

Trading gives him "emotions" – it's similar to Jane's story. It's a sign he's not really treating it as a business. He is treating trading as a lifestyle. But it *isn't* a lifestyle: it's a business!

The main reason he will never make money is, as he admits, he finds it hard to take a loss. I think not taking losses comes from anxiousness to prove that he is right. After so long he wants more than ever to prove that he can be a success. I'm afraid that's another reason it is unlikely to happen.

 In both cases neither trader had bothered to research that nearly everyone loses trying to day trade currencies. Or if they had researched it, they didn't want to know the truth.

Would it be possible for either to become a shark and succeed?

Both would have to forget trading currencies and put some work into learning how to trade shares for the long term. Jane would need her own computer and desk away from the kids. Her lifestyle was probably too busy for any sort of frequent trading – her best bet would be as a buy-and-hold investor. But that isn't going to make her the big bucks quickly (though it can make very big bucks in the end if you buy the right stocks and leave them alone). The antiques dealer has an outside chance. But he would have to change strategy completely and learn to take his losses.

Both stories show the negative role played by emotions. They are the main thing we have to cut out if we want to be sharks. I hope to persuade you of this during this book – and show you how to do it. You don't want to be a Jane – a dreamer with no plan and no idea. Or the guy doing it for seven years for nothing.

"If your edge puts the odds in your favour, then every loss puts you that much closer to a win. When you really believe this, your response to a losing trade will no longer take on a negative emotional quality."

Mark Douglas

What Kind of Trader Are You?

As a trader it's important to have a good understanding of your character in order to get closer to the shark ideal. You have to take a good look at yourself – what emotions do you have that could stop you making money? What part of your brain needs to be decluttered?

In *The Naked Trader* I have a chapter like this looking at the broad types of trader and investor you find in the markets. Here I want to focus exclusively on the psychological side of things.

We all have an emotional brain – our emotions drive us to achieve things in life. But to succeed in trading we have to know which emotions are likely to cause us trouble and avoid them.

Let me sum up the types of market character that I have seen over the years and how emotions affect their trading.

Which of these could you be? Where do you recognise yourself? Most of us probably see ourselves in more than one. Have a think.

It's the beginning of figuring out the problems you might encounter turning shark.

Lovers

Lovers totally fall for one or two companies. They really love them and can't understand why no one else feels the love. If you went out with a lover they would be really hard to dump. Lovers simply refuse to believe no one feels the love for their favoured companies, and carry on buying regardless of negatives – certain that others will soon see the love is not misplaced.

I have met many lovers (Oo-er – Ed.) and believe me: the look on their face when describing their favourite share really is the same as a look of love. I remember one in particular. "Rockhopper", he kept saying. "This one is worth at least treble." He kept regaling me with stories of how he and Rockhopper had walked hand in hand through perfumed gardens... It was pointless trying to suggest Rockhopper had some very bad habits (like not finding much oil). And of course Rockhopper inevitably sank.

He's probably still writing love notes to Rockhopper.

The thing about trading is that you have to be prepared to divorce your shares.

Out-of-the-boxers

Out of the boxers and straight into bed is how my wife likes it... but that's not what we're here to talk about.

Out-of-the-boxers are those people who try and think – yes – out of the box. Instead of going for simple trades they want to do weird things. And then when they get bored they want to do even weirder things. So they ask about binaries and options and straddles and bonds and trusts and Bollinger Bands. They just can't imagine doing anything normal. It's not interesting enough.

They get caught up in all kinds of technical trades, getting ever deeper into the complexities. This usually ends up being frustrating for them. They can't figure out why 'out of the box' thinking isn't working. But it usually doesn't.

They are the same characters who spend work meetings boring on about stuff that no one is interested in (come on – it's lunchtime, shut up!). I had an out-of-the-boxer at a seminar once who wanted to discuss 'dark pools' and he didn't mean swimming with the lights off.

A trade isn't more likely to succeed because it is complicated, original or obscure, especially if you only half grasp what on earth you're doing. Be logical!

Gamblers

"Many short-term players view trading as a form of gambling. Without planning or discipline, they throw money at the market. The occasional big score reinforces this easy money attitude but sets them up for ultimate failure. Without defensive rules, insiders easily feed off these losers and send them off to other hobbies."

Alan Farley

Gamblers just can't help it. They need continual excitement and stimulation (don't get involved with them personally, you'll get worn out). They move from one gamble to the next. They aren't really interested in researching much – they simply can't wait for the next fix. That buzz of pressing the buy button.

They even enjoy it if a gamble goes wrong – they can have a moan about it with their gambling pals. Wrong or right, they just want the thrill of the game, which is fine if they want a buzz but not if they want to make money.

They're also likely to take profits too fast (again for the thrill) and to day trade for even bigger rushes.

Worriers

Worriers worry about everything, all the time. Worry, worry, worry – they just aren't happy unless they can worry about something. They worry about every trade, and more often worry so much about putting them on that they don't place them at all. If they eventually get round to placing a trade, they worry about it so much they get out too fast.

There are all sorts of ways to protect yourself from losses as a trader – but worrying isn't one of them.

Perfectionists

Perfectionists are so determined to get everything right that they end up failing because they don't realise the market isn't a perfect mechanism. (It's just as well it isn't or it would be a bit hard to make any money.)

I remember one perfectionist I once met. He couldn't understand why it wasn't possible to get an exact valuation on a share. In effect he wanted the *right answer* – when there isn't one! There is no such thing as perfection in the markets.

I bet this chap's house was perfect, with the cushions all just so. It's not possible with stocks: the market is always a total mess and you have to trade like a shark to make sense of it.

Sheep

Sheep are way too easily led. They can't buy anything unless their favourite tipster/bulletin board/Twitter account/website told them to or said they were buying in. The sheep pile in behind but unfortunately forget their favoured leader might disappear if anything goes wrong, leaving them sitting in their own doo-doo.

Lazy bums

The lazy bums believe the ads that tell them they can make a zillion pounds in five minutes by following a new amazing system. They believe what almost anyone tells them because it means they can stick a few quid on without having to bother doing any research or work. They are too lazy to sell when they should and too lazy to have any kind of plan. The only way they'll become a shark is a sharp boot up the bum.

Whatever you do in life – unless you get lucky and win the lottery ("It *won't* be you!") – if you want to succeed you have to work at it. Even if you are naturally talented at something, there is practice, rehearsal, dedication; success doesn't come out of nowhere. It is the same with trading.

Mules

Mules are the opposite of sheep. They're just as bad but in a different way: they are insanely stubborn. They take a position, know they are right, and no one can say anything to make them change their minds. They often combine it with a knowing look.

I remember one chap who came to a seminar. He liked Tesco shares and had bought them at what he thought was the bargain price of 320p.

"You can't possibly go wrong buying the shares of a big supermarket," he said. "Everyone needs to eat. I intend to keep these for years."

"What if people go and find stuff to eat at other supermarkets?" I asked.

He did a French shrug of the shoulders thing and gave me a look so knowing he might as well have been smoking a pipe and wearing a tweed jacket with leather patches on the elbows.

I bet he still has them now after they have dropped by almost 50%.

Cats

By cats I don't mind a kind of jazz club regular (Oooh, you cool cat). I'm thinking of the way that cats stalk small animals for ages – finally grab them – and then... get bored.

There are quite a few traders like this. They stalk their trades, enjoy doing the research and getting the right price, enjoy the thrill of the chase and then... lose interest.

At least they don't sell up automatically. Cats often get the longer-term winners because of this – through sheer boredom. But they also let their losses run.

I think cats could be turned into sharks quite simply – just by getting them to add in stop-losses to all their trades. If they do that, cats could be brilliant. Get bored with your trades? Get to know trailing stops! (Now you really are a cool cat, honest.)

Ponies

Ponies only have one trick, usually the strategy they adopted as newcomers to the market. And even if it loses them money they carry on with it regardless.

If their method works at the start it can be very hard for them to change – they become absolutely certain that the one trick is for them. I remember a trader who just bought the biggest losers. It worked for a bit as they all recovered slightly. Then he got badly stuck. A big loser became an even bigger loser (amazingly). He didn't know what to do.

I persuaded him to be more like Mr Spock. It took a while – but his ears have turned pointy and he shows every sign of enjoying trading success in future.

Greedy guts

Feeling greedy is a pretty strong human emotion. After all, you're reading this book in the hope it will help make you some money, and there's nothing wrong with that – we are all susceptible to a little bit of greed. But the more eager you are to make money quickly, the less likely you are to make it.

Greedy guts trade way too often and look for ways to make big money fast – which normally ends up in a whole heap of bad mistakes.

Sharks

Yes, I have come across actual trading sharks. Cold-blooded, ruthless, logical, the ideal traders. Some lucky people come to the markets as sharks already. But it's rare. Most sharks had to journey towards it. They were the other characters you've read about. And that's fine – that's most of us. No one has to be stuck as a gambling greedy guts mule all their days (where did I put my Twix stash?).

As private investors and traders we have it easy in that respect. In a couple of chapters I'll be looking at a fascinating study of full-time professional investors. Any one of them with bad habits can really struggle to change: it's too hard to shift when there is a lot of money to manage.

But as private investors and traders we are – that's right – running our own businesses.

We're our own damn bosses.

We can change if we want to!

I have seen people turn from gamblers and out-of-boxers and cats to sharks. I want this book to help you, no matter which combination of characters you are, to do the same.

I now class myself as a shark – but I wasn't always that way. And even now it's only most of the time. When I have non-shark moments I recognise them. The giveaway is usually shouting bad words I shouldn't know at the screen (I picked them up from football fans).

Some real-life sharks

Here are some people I would consider to be sharks.

This isn't necessarily a good thing in life as a whole. Often the best traders are actually not very nice. After all, some of the best traders are bankers.

In fact, the truth is: to be a good trader... you need to be a total bastard. (Let me make it clear: a total bastard only when you are trading!)

There is no room for emotion whatsoever. To win you have to take money from people with emotion.

Baron Sugar

Yes, that guy from *The Apprentice*. Thinks like a complete tosspot when it comes to his investments, he doesn't care about anything but making money.

I am sure he is nice to people that really know him but in business he doesn't care who he tramples on to get what he wants and it is the figures or likely figures he is after. He don't like no bullshit and if you are trading I am afraid you will have to act a bit like him.

"You're fired!" is what you need to say to your badly performing shares.

Donald Trump

Frankly he comes across like a total jerk whatever he does or says (and what's with the hair?). As a businessman? He'd trample you into the dirt just like that to get what he wanted. And in the shares market, I'm afraid you have to trample on others (but only electronically). If you win, those on the other end of your trade lose.

Tony Blair

Totally ruthless. Like pretending to Gordon Brown he'd stand down ASAP to let him be PM. Will do anything he can to get his way. Scheming – yes, you have to scheme a bit.

I know, it is hard – to be a good trader you do need to be a bit Blairish (sorry).

Peter Jones

The *Dragons' Den* guy. If you come onto the show with a valuation of £2m for your new business selling gourmet pork scratchings (Hey, that's a good idea, don't publish this bit – Robbie) and you sold 100 packs and made a tenner don't expect anything else but short shrift.

He wouldn't buy a business that is obviously overvalued on any kind of sensible valuation. That's why – like Peter – you should always look at the figures. (And as his hair turns greyer expect him to buy a hair dye company.)

Vladimir Putin

No problem at all – master trader and 100% shark. I suppose the only thing is that he might have a problem focusing as he is very busy doing some very bad— ooops, hang on, who's that shady character coming up the path to the house? – I mean some very good things, he is so handsome and virile and…

James Bond

As long as he avoids getting either shaken or stirred, he'd be a master trader. Cool decisions are what are needed under pressure.

I suspect he would spy out some excellent opportunities. (Shoots self. – Ed.)

Some real-life non-sharks

Nick Leeson

You simply cannot lose the plot. Nick Leeson, the man who managed to bring down one of the world's oldest banks in a fit of crazy gambling, is a great example of a non-shark.

When things started to go wrong and he lost heavily he should have told his bosses, stopped and maybe then he had a chance to start again. Instead, not only did he lose the plot, he hid his losses in fake accounts. He really thought he could win some of the money back. (He couldn't.)

Jeremy Corbyn

If you're buying this book in the bargain bucket some time in the future you may not remember him. Leaving aside the fact that he would like to dismantle the stock market, he'd be awful. He'd be trampled over by everyone else days before he decided to make a decision on something. Also, all his family and friends would be asked to vote whether he should buy or sell a stock, with the final decision going to "Wayne from Clapham".

Gordon Brown

Don't you miss him? What terrible clanger was he going to make next? I do miss that. Unbelievably he was in charge of our economy for almost ten years – it was no wonder we got into a mess. What a terrible trader he'd be – very far from a shark.

This whole book could be about how to avoid his characteristics to be a good trader. From violent fits of temper, to wrongly placed arrogance – "no more boom or bust" just as we were about to bust. And the classic – selling shares right at the bottom (in his case he sold our gold right at the bottom). Too many mixed emotions and arrogance together, Gordon would soon have a zero balance.

Managing
Your Trades

If you have ever run a business you'll know that one of the most important things to keep an eye on is how you manage things – money, staff, products. It's no surprise, then, that managing your trades is key to successful trading.

In this chapter we'll cover how to manage your trades: from getting the basics right, through to how to open and close trades with all the calm and logic of Mr Spock on a beach recliner reading Aristotle.

"If there is such a thing as a secret to the nature of trading, this is it: At the very core of one's ability 1) to trade without fear or overconfidence, 2) perceive what the market is offering from its perspective, 3) stay completely focused in the 'now moment opportunity flow,' and 4) spontaneously enter the 'zone,' is a strong, virtually unshakeable belief in an uncertain outcome with an edge in your favour."

Mark Douglas

The basics

Trade tax-free

Logical traders always want to trade tax-free – after all, it's only logical. So they always use their ISA allowance every year (or as much of it as they can afford). They also use spread betting (though differently to their ISA – as we'll explore later).

The government gives you a capital gains tax allowance of £11,000 a year as I write, so you could also make that much profit, taking out costs, outside of ISAs and spread bets and still pay no tax.

Bank profits

A business is all about making profits – and I think profits should be 'banked', especially from spread betting accounts. And when I say banked – I mean they should be set aside in bonds, premium bonds, savings or property. I have put money into each of those (and made some profits, but that wasn't the main objective).

The temptation is to plough all profits back into the business, but logically it does not make sense. Much better to bank. Otherwise you could end up risking all the gains. Once the gains are put away into safe havens they really become gains.

Destroy all debts

Before anything else, logical traders pay off their debts/mortgages. They consider it human folly to keep borrowing because interest rates are low. They will not be low forever and debts have to be paid sometime. Once you are debt-free you really can trade like a shark.

Logical traders aren't tight; life is to be enjoyed – but they disapprove of contactless cards. That just enables more people to get into more debt by buying more expensive coffees they can't really afford. They believe it is much better to use cash – money you can really see.

The human lifespan has lengthened and it will be increasingly normal for people to live into their 90s. That could leave 30 years of retirement. Who wants to start retirement with a massive debt? Always pay off debt.

Trade with what you can afford to lose

Trading like a shark is easiest when you are trading with money you can afford to lose and are honest with yourself about that. If you have, say, £20,000 invested, will you be OK if only £5,000 is left? Did you really need that £20,000?

Think of the money being 'ring-fenced' – or do what I do, pretend you don't actually have any of it. It's already gone. (It's also brilliant if anyone asks me for a tenner.) Now treating it as a business should be easier.

"I know of a few millionaires who started trading with inherited wealth. In each case, they lost it all because they didn't feel the pain when they were losing. In those formative first years of trading, they felt they could afford to lose. You're much better off going into the market on a shoestring, feeling that you can't afford to lose. I'd rather bet on somebody starting out with a few thousand dollars than on somebody who came in with millions ... This is one of the few industries where you can still engineer a rags-to-riches story. Richard Dennis started out with only hundreds of dollars and ended up making hundreds of millions in less than two decades – that's quite motivating."

William Eckhardt

Trades in action

There are a lot of examples of shares I have bought and why – and what happened next – in my other two books and on my website at **www.nakedtrader.co.uk**. But I think it's worth just having a look at one or two trades to show how sharks can win or lose from a trade while non-sharks just lose.

"The 'making money' part of trading is simply a by-product (end result) of a focused and precise utilization of our trained psychological and mechanical resources to successfully find and manage trades. Under the most intense circumstances, the best results will be produced only with a deep concentration and focus on the task at hand."

Chris Lori

Trade 1: Pets at Home

After some logical research, I thought shares in Pets At Home looked cheap in October 2014. They had had a dog of a time but they looked like good value. I bought in at 171p. (In fact I made this trade live at a seminar.)

Unemotionally, I had to consider at the same time: what if I am wrong? What if the shares are down because Pets at Home is, well, a dog?

So here is my shark – or Spock-like – plan in action. I bought 5,000 shares at 171p in October 2014. The chart showed they had been sitting around 170–175p for some time, finding plenty of support. Logically, if they started falling below 170p, the shares would likely resume a downwards motion. So I decided to monitor things closely and get out fast if shares fell below 168p. That would leave me with a total potential loss of £150. Additionally, I placed a stop-loss at 162 just in case the shares suddenly shot a lot lower.

If it goes up? Sharks love running profits. I had no upper target in mind just yet; I wanted to see what happened. But I wasn't looking to grab a small, quick profit. It's not a logical way to make a lot of money.

So, a small loss if I get it wrong, run profits if it goes up – and see what happens.

What happened next? The shares stayed where they were for a bit but never got to my get-out-quick loss. They then went up to 200p. At that point a shark mind says – put a stop-loss in at 171p. If the worst comes to worst, the trade won't lose.

The shares stayed at 200p-ish for ages then started to move up. I moved the stop up to 200p. The shares slowly rose to 300p. I moved the stop up to 250p.

The shares fell a bit but I was still in there. Eventually they hit the dizzy heights of 312! With such a good gain, I sold half and moved the stop on the rest to 295. The shares fell, the 295 got hit and I was out. My profit was over £6,500. Not bad. It took about a year.

Using the stop meant that once it was up past 220p I could just let the trade ride out to its ultimate conclusion without any further work. Sharktastic!

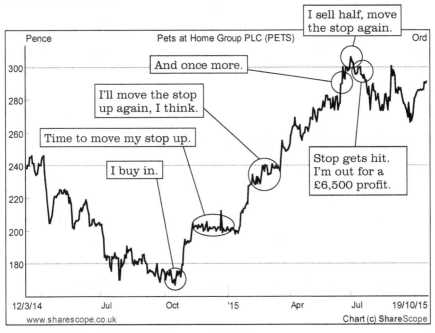

Pets at Home – a sharktastic trade

take a small loss if the trade goes wrong. I'm not yet sure what my target is but perhaps there is 20% upside from here. I'm in at 35p.

Non-shark: These shares have tanked. They've got to come back! I looked at Twitter and this bloke on there – HotTrader – really knows his stuff and he's in. So I'm buying big – watch this fly. In at 35!

SHARES HIT 38p

Shark: Excellent – this trade is going well. It looks like there's more upside on the way – but I have to remember this is a risky one. Now the shares are nicely higher I can try and make sure this trade never loses. I'll put in a stop-loss at 35p, same as my entry point. If the shares go back I'll be out at break-even.

Non-shark: Told ya! I'm going on Twitter to say nice one HotTrader! I reckon this could double from here. I just checked the bulletin boards and they are all buying more. I'm going to buy a shedload more at 38. It feels good pressing the buy button on a trade this certain – I am so excited about this one.

SHARES HEAD BACK TO 35p

Shark: I sold at 35.5, just before my stop got hit because I checked supply and demand on level 2 and it looked weak. I am out with a small profit. This trade failed. I am going to keep a watching brief on the company and see what happens next. I must be aware not to get emotionally involved with the share and start trying to play it unless I am sure it is a good trade again.

Non-shark: S***! HotTrader never expected it to go down. He just said on Twitter that it's a double bottom on the chart, which is great news! Same with the guys on the bulletin boards. I am in for more and going to average down, two lots at 35p and one lot at 38p, building a great trade right here!

take a small loss if the trade goes wrong. I'm not yet sure what my target is but perhaps there is 20% upside from here. I'm in at 35p.

Non-shark: These shares have tanked. They've got to come back! I looked at Twitter and this bloke on there – HotTrader – really knows his stuff and he's in. So I'm buying big – watch this fly. In at 35!

SHARES HIT 38p

Shark: Excellent – this trade is going well. It looks like there's more upside on the way – but I have to remember this is a risky one. Now the shares are nicely higher I can try and make sure this trade never loses. I'll put in a stop-loss at 35p, same as my entry point. If the shares go back I'll be out at break-even.

Non-shark: Told ya! I'm going on Twitter to say nice one HotTrader! I reckon this could double from here. I just checked the bulletin boards and they are all buying more. I'm going to buy a shedload more at 38. It feels good pressing the buy button on a trade this certain – I am so excited about this one.

SHARES HEAD BACK TO 35p

Shark: I sold at 35.5, just before my stop got hit because I checked supply and demand on level 2 and it looked weak. I am out with a small profit. This trade failed. I am going to keep a watching brief on the company and see what happens next. I must be aware not to get emotionally involved with the share and start trying to play it unless I am sure it is a good trade again.

Non-shark: S***! HotTrader never expected it to go down. He just said on Twitter that it's a double bottom on the chart, which is great news! Same with the guys on the bulletin boards. I am in for more and going to average down, two lots at 35p and one lot at 38p, building a great trade right here!

way or not. To illustrate the importance of getting into the right mode *before* trading, here's a detailed run-through of the difference between how a Vulcan and a non-Vulcan (or shark and non-shark) open a trade... leading to a totally different result.

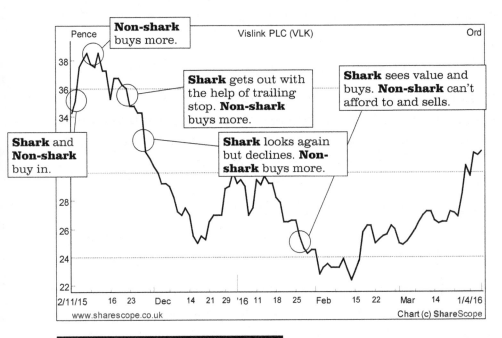

www.sharescope.co.uk

Chart (c) ShareScope

Vislink – a visually tempting trade

Vislink shares are at 35p, having already dropped a fair way. They look like pretty good value.

Shark: This company looks interesting – but it has come down quite a lot for a reason. So I must be cautious. I don't want to be holding the shares if they carry on going down.

Management is under the cosh from shareholders for awarding itself a generous share deal and there are some question marks over the company's progress. With risk here, I'll keep any stake small just in case.

I've checked level 2 and can see there are buyers around, which means good support at 35p. I am going to set a stop-loss at 32p and

Trade 2: Pets at Home (!)

This second trade didn't work – and it's, er, the very same company!

In March 2014 Pets at Home was floated on the stock market for the first time. Near to this time – seven months or so before my successful trade in the company – I bought 2,000 shares at 235.5p. As a good shark, I had a get-out-quick stop. The get-out-quick kicked in at 229 and I lost £130.

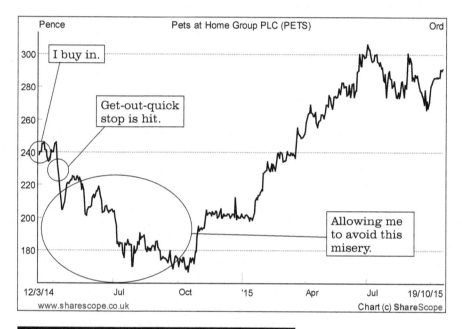

Pets at Home – the power of the panic stop

As we now know it went all the way down to 171! Of course, you could argue if I had held on for months eventually it would have turned a profit – but psychologically it is not wise to have big losers staring at you in a portfolio. A shark gets rid of them pronto.

Opening a trade through the eyes of a shark and a non-shark

As you can see, planning from the get-go is vital. How you open a trade is a big indication of whether you are doing things the right

So, a small loss if I get it wrong, run profits if it goes up – and see what happens.

What happened next? The shares stayed where they were for a bit but never got to my get-out-quick loss. They then went up to 200p. At that point a shark mind says – put a stop-loss in at 171p. If the worst comes to worst, the trade won't lose.

The shares stayed at 200p-ish for ages then started to move up. I moved the stop up to 200p. The shares slowly rose to 300p. I moved the stop up to 250p.

The shares fell a bit but I was still in there. Eventually they hit the dizzy heights of 312! With such a good gain, I sold half and moved the stop on the rest to 295. The shares fell, the 295 got hit and I was out. My profit was over £6,500. Not bad. It took about a year.

Using the stop meant that once it was up past 220p I could just let the trade ride out to its ultimate conclusion without any further work. Sharktastic!

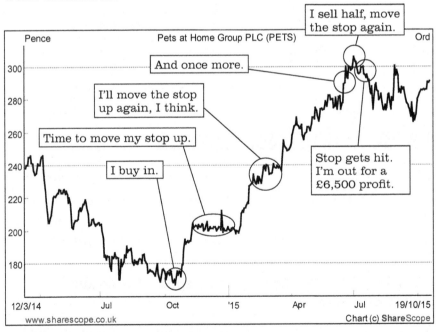

Pets at Home – a sharktastic trade

at **www.nakedtrader.co.uk**. But I think it's worth just having a look at one or two trades to show how sharks can win or lose from a trade while non-sharks just lose.

"The 'making money' part of trading is simply a by-product (end result) of a focused and precise utilization of our trained psychological and mechanical resources to successfully find and manage trades. Under the most intense circumstances, the best results will be produced only with a deep concentration and focus on the task at hand."

Chris Lori

Trade 1: Pets at Home

After some logical research, I thought shares in Pets At Home looked cheap in October 2014. They had had a dog of a time but they looked like good value. I bought in at 171p. (In fact I made this trade live at a seminar.)

Unemotionally, I had to consider at the same time: what if I am wrong? What if the shares are down because Pets at Home is, well, a dog?

So here is my shark – or Spock-like – plan in action. I bought 5,000 shares at 171p in October 2014. The chart showed they had been sitting around 170–175p for some time, finding plenty of support. Logically, if they started falling below 170p, the shares would likely resume a downwards motion. So I decided to monitor things closely and get out fast if shares fell below 168p. That would leave me with a total potential loss of £150. Additionally, I placed a stop-loss at 162 just in case the shares suddenly shot a lot lower.

If it goes up? Sharks love running profits. I had no upper target in mind just yet; I wanted to see what happened. But I wasn't looking to grab a small, quick profit. It's not a logical way to make a lot of money.

The human lifespan has lengthened and it will be increasingly normal for people to live into their 90s. That could leave 30 years of retirement. Who wants to start retirement with a massive debt? Always pay off debt.

Trade with what you can afford to lose

Trading like a shark is easiest when you are trading with money you can afford to lose and are honest with yourself about that. If you have, say, £20,000 invested, will you be OK if only £5,000 is left? Did you really need that £20,000?

Think of the money being 'ring-fenced' – or do what I do, pretend you don't actually have any of it. It's already gone. (It's also brilliant if anyone asks me for a tenner.) Now treating it as a business should be easier.

"I know of a few millionaires who started trading with inherited wealth. In each case, they lost it all because they didn't feel the pain when they were losing. In those formative first years of trading, they felt they could afford to lose. You're much better off going into the market on a shoestring, feeling that you can't afford to lose. I'd rather bet on somebody starting out with a few thousand dollars than on somebody who came in with millions ... This is one of the few industries where you can still engineer a rags-to-riches story. Richard Dennis started out with only hundreds of dollars and ended up making hundreds of millions in less than two decades – that's quite motivating."

William Eckhardt

Trades in action

There are a lot of examples of shares I have bought and why – and what happened next – in my other two books and on my website

SHARES GO DOWN TO 31P

Shark: Let's have another look. No, there's a lot of sellers around. The market as a whole is tumbling. I'll leave it for now.

Non-shark: What a bargain this is now! HotTrader says this can't go any lower and it's only because the market has been hit and people are selling even good stuff. Time to buy a final lot. I'm going to take giant profits once it is back to 65p.

SHARES GO TO 25p

Shark: The shares appear to have bottomed out. Some buyers are starting to come back in. However, this still is high-risk – though less risky than at 35p. Given the buying and the cheapness I'll buy small at 25p. But given the risk, I will be out fast at 23p.

Non-shark: I've had to dump these and take a loss of £3,000. The market's in meltdown and I'm selling everything. At least I'll get some money back. HotTrader hasn't mentioned these shares for a while. I wonder what he's doing with them. A lot of posters seem to have vanished from the bulletin boards. Bloody market, bloody shares. I'm thinking of giving up totally – the world is going to hell.

Recovery play perils

Rockhopper is a classic recent example of a potential 'recovery play' – one of those opportunities that non-sharks think can't possibly go wrong. Until it does. If you want to remember the most important lessons of this chapter, photocopy this chart and pin it above your trading desk:

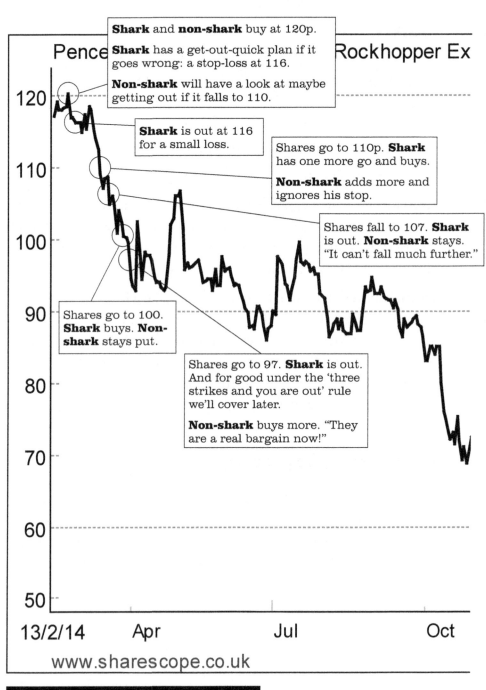

Shark and **non-shark** buy at 120p.

Shark has a get-out-quick plan if it goes wrong: a stop-loss at 116.

Non-shark will have a look at maybe getting out if it falls to 110.

Shark is out at 116 for a small loss.

Shares go to 110p. **Shark** has one more go and buys.

Non-shark adds more and ignores his stop.

Shares fall to 107. **Shark** is out. **Non-shark** stays. "It can't fall much further."

Shares go to 100. **Shark** buys. **Non-shark** stays put.

Shares go to 97. **Shark** is out. And for good under the 'three strikes and you are out' rule we'll cover later.

Non-shark buys more. "They are a real bargain now!"

Pence ... Rockhopper Ex

120

110

100

90

80

70

60

50

13/2/14   Apr   Jul   Oct

www.sharescope.co.uk

Rockhopper – rock on or hopping mad?

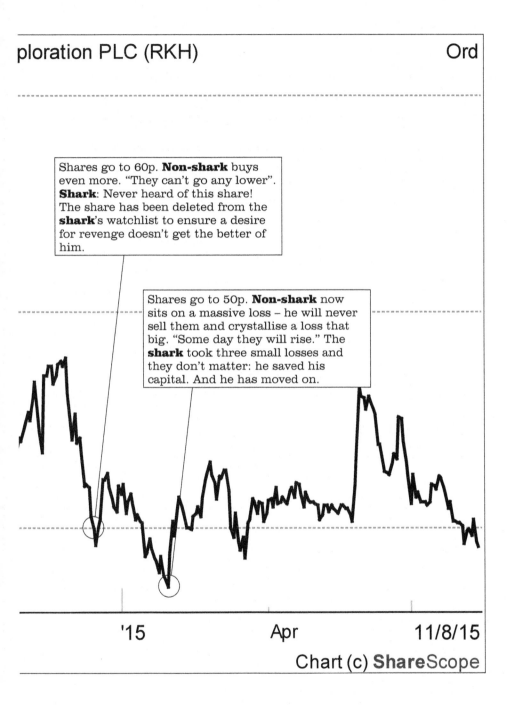

ploration PLC (RKH)   Ord

Shares go to 60p. **Non-shark** buys even more. "They can't go any lower". **Shark**: Never heard of this share! The share has been deleted from the **shark**'s watchlist to ensure a desire for revenge doesn't get the better of him.

Shares go to 50p. **Non-shark** now sits on a massive loss – he will never sell them and crystallise a loss that big. "Some day they will rise." The **shark** took three small losses and they don't matter: he saved his capital. And he has moved on.

'15   Apr   11/8/15

Chart (c) **Share**Scope

The lessons of these trades? Have a plan! Know when you are getting out and why. Don't let losses get too big.

These examples are there to show you how trading like a shark should work in managing your trades. If we are trading we want to make money and not lose it. We want to make as much as we can so we want to run the profits if possible and cut losses fast.

We know it is never possible to time everything to perfection. But hopefully we can always protect our capital and get one or two very big wins.

Trading in Down Markets

The market is falling. Headlines in the papers are all doom and gloom: "Bear market rages". "Market crash warning". "Sell everything says Bank".

Twitter is all a-twitter. Traders are all in a panic.

What does trading like a shark mean at such a time?

When all the world is falling down

Someone who trades like a shark:

- Has probably lightened up on some positions as the market falls.

- Totally ignores the media headlines.

- Will concentrate on his positions and take logical steps.

- Is already in some cash; he knows there is a chance his shares could fall further but also knows it costs quite a bit to sell things and then buy them back.

- Turns to short spread bets and short ETFs to mitigate his risk. (ETFs are exchange-traded funds. For more on these see my book *The Naked Trader* where I go through some worked examples.) He uses a clever ETF that goes up by two or three times the amount the FTSE 100 goes down[1] and sets his trade up with stops so that he can't lose more than he puts in. If the FTSE smashes down, he could make a massive percentage on the ETF. Once it begins to recover he could bank those gains and start to buy back in.

- Knows it is hard to make money when the market is panicking and going down as even his good stuff will head down in the chaos.

- Doesn't expect to make a lot short-term but is happy to only lose a small amount and get ready for the market turn. Then he will buy and start to exit the shorts.

- Doesn't panic or think it is the end of the world. He knows newspapers sell on fear and plenty of magazines do too. And social media often echoes it meaninglessly.

- Ignores all the 'experts' that pop up on TV looking concerned. He also ignores all the stock footage of traders looking terrified with their hands on their heads. That is is just silly, hysterical stuff.

- Is only interested in following the market down or up slowly and cautiously. He is not interested in second-guessing what is going to happen next or in the near term.

If the crash story has reached the headlines then a lot of the fall has probably already happened.

A non-shark:

- Is in total panic mode.

- Can hardly believe that all his shares just keep going down.

---

1   ETFX FTSE 100 super-short strategy (2x) FD. (Memorable, eh?)

- Waits and waits but the market keeps falling and after losing a lot he starts selling.

- Finds it difficult to sell some of the high-risk penny shares he has bought. The market makers don't want them and offer him prices well below the published prices; he never knew they are allowed to do that for smaller shares.

- In a panic remembers about shorting but just sticks on spread bets – with stop-losses, but the market is so volatile his stops get taken out.

- Doesn't know about short ETFs.

The market starts to turn but now he is full of fear and just can't bring himself to buy anything in case it all happens again.

Shorting

Bear markets are tough on everyone. Even the best traders can lose the plot. Trying to run the winners might stop working – because there are no winners!

When that happens, there might only be one logical way to make money: shorting.

When a shark sees the market tumbling he knows a few things:

- It might well keep tumbling – but it could equally turn around as quickly as it went down.

- It is impossible for anyone to know or call an exact top or bottom regardless of how clever they might look on Bloomberg.

- He must consider changing his business plan slowly but surely.

- He must accept that, for a while anyway, he might not make much money – but the most important thing is not to lose much.

He looks at the FTSE chart for the past 50 years and can see that if he was out of the market during the short but sharp bear years he would have enjoyed serious success. But he also knows he has to be in for when the market shifts up and that's too hard to judge.

What to do? The shark puzzles over this and comes to a logical (indeed very Spock-like) conclusion: keep holding good companies in which he is still up (or not down by much), drop any stinkers ASAP, and go short on either some shares or the FTSE index itself in order to hedge his losses.

By selling losing shares quickly he has cut his potential losses and also has cash on hand ready to buy when the upturn starts.

He knows it is impossible to get in at tops and bottoms – he just needs a ride the right way for part of the journey.

All the angles

Like any good businessman, a shark knows that running a business entails trying to make money from all the angles you can.

I used to own and run a café in London. When I bought it it was selling coffee, cake and snacks – making a reasonable profit. But the previous owner wasn't making the most of it by a long chalk.

I soon added cooked breakfasts. Then good lunches for the local office workers. More money flowed in. How about DVD rentals? They worked too: I rented them cheap so people came in the evening to pick up takeaway meals. I used A-boards outside with different posters for different times of the day.

I also cut costs by shopping around for services. In the end I sold the whole place for double what I paid for it. I explored every possible way to make the most profit. The same is needed in trading: if you run it as a business you need to use all the tools at your disposal.

And that should include shorting. When shares tumble, selling up is very costly. Shorting allows you to hold onto your shares, waiting for the turnaround, while making money from the markets going down.

It is so easy these days to go short with spread betting. It's even tax-free. But when I talk to the industry they tell me hardly any private investors ever go short.

Perhaps it is because people find it difficult. Some people have told me it just feels weird to make money from something going down. I ask them how they intend to make money if we have a bear market. They usually shrug.

That is really not looking at trading as a business. It makes no sense not to be able to make money on rainy days.

I made a massive amount shorting Carpetright. My short made no difference to the share really – I don't think I put anyone out of a job. It's just that it was only making £8m and was valued at £400m which made absolutely no sense. I ended up making more than £25,000 by backing the shares to go down from 740p to 315p, at which point I exited the short. Then I shorted it again from 615p to 400p.

Going short on Carpetright

The company just happened to be overvalued. There was nothing terribly wrong with it, it just sold carpets. But it seems silly not to be able to make money from it by not having the potential to go short.

The results of a $1bn experiment

Lee Freeman-Shor runs over a billion dollars worth of funds. The way he invests is by giving the world's best investors millions to invest – but only in up to ten of their very best ideas.

That must be a recipe for success, right?

Well, after seven years, he examined his investors' 1,866 investments. He found that most of their investments *lost* money. These great fund managers were only right 30% of the time. Nevertheless, overall most of them made significant profits.

Freeman-Shor wanted to find out how something so remarkable was possible. He started digging through the data. His results were fascinating. It turned out that winning as a trader or investor wasn't about being right all of the time – or even most of the time. It was all about how you execute your trades. That's why he called his book about this *The Art of Execution*.

It's not a guide for would-be jihadis, honest – they'd be rubbish traders (always blowing up their accounts).

The five tribes

After studying their behaviour and results, Freeman-Shor split his fund managers into five tribes: Rabbits, Assassins, Hunters, Raiders and Connoisseurs.

I think all traders can learn how to be more shark-like by looking at what these tribes did right and wrong.

The Rabbits

The Rabbits were the worst and ended up being fired. Rabbit mistakes were ones sharks would not countenance: holding onto losers, in particular. Their egos wouldn't let them sell. They didn't

How the Professionals Do it

So to be a good trader you need to run it like a business. What about those traders or investors who actually do trade and invest for real-life businesses – the pros in the City or on Wall Street?

Do they have anything they can teach us home traders as we sit in our underpants watching them run to catch packed trains into work? (£8,000 a year for the space beneath Mr Jones's left armpit, a snip at the price!) Beneath their bowler hats, do there lurk shark fins (or Vulcan ears)?

Luckily one fund manager has done the research for us and shared the secrets of the professionals' success – or lack of it.

The company just happened to be overvalued. There was nothing terribly wrong with it, it just sold carpets. But it seems silly not to be able to make money from it by not having the potential to go short.

It is so easy these days to go short with spread betting. It's even tax-free. But when I talk to the industry they tell me hardly any private investors ever go short.

Perhaps it is because people find it difficult. Some people have told me it just feels weird to make money from something going down. I ask them how they intend to make money if we have a bear market. They usually shrug.

That is really not looking at trading as a business. It makes no sense not to be able to make money on rainy days.

I made a massive amount shorting Carpetright. My short made no difference to the share really – I don't think I put anyone out of a job. It's just that it was only making £8m and was valued at £400m which made absolutely no sense. I ended up making more than £25,000 by backing the shares to go down from 740p to 315p, at which point I exited the short. Then I shorted it again from 615p to 400p.

Going short on Carpetright

like being wrong and suffered from gambler's fallacy ("I am due a win").

Rabbits tended to be alpha males and over-confident. They never said, "I don't know". Many held onto shares for too long.

They also had fear of the unknown – if they sold out there could be a rally and they would miss out. Better the devil you know.

Rabbits may have pointy ears but they were nothing like sharks.

The Assassins

The Assassins were ruthless at selling losing positions to preserve capital – shooting underperforming shares in the back of the head like professional hitmen. They set stops at between 20 and 33% so they didn't get whipsawed out and could still recover if the price went back up.

They also knew that time is money so they killed stocks that didn't move for some time (around six months). A cold-hearted bunch!

Finally, when taking a loss they were careful not to invest too quickly just because the cash was there. They waited for the next opportunity.

The Hunters

The Hunters bought loads more shares after a price had gone *down*. But this was planned when they bought the first lot (rather than in a panicky attempt to reduce losses in the hope of a share turning around). They were value investors stalking their prey.

The Raiders

The Raiders were terrified of losing everything. Once in profit they liked to bank it. One Raider had a 70% hit rate at picking winners but *still* lost money. His profits never amounted to enough to offset the losses of the other 30%.

The Connoisseurs

The Connoisseurs treated every investment like a vintage wine. If it was off, they got rid of it immediately. But if it was good they knew it would only get better with age. They took small profits off the top to please some of their investors but left the rest to mature.

Amazingly the Connoisseurs had the worst record as stock pickers: six out of ten investments they made would lose. But when they won, they won big. And they built up big positions in the winners.

Apparently Freeman-Shor's meetings with the Connoisseurs were very boring because there was usually so little to report.

A shark's execution

Freeman-Shor's research goes to show the truth of what market legend George Soros said: "It is not whether you are right or wrong that is important but how much money you make when you are right and how much you lose when you're wrong."

And that is exactly what sharks are after: not minding about how many losses they make as long as they aren't too big. And finding some really big profits from a small number of trades that really go right.

Where would sharks fall among Lee's tribes? I think they'd mostly be Connoisseurs. While some of the other tribes have merit, emotion could be much more of an obstacle for them.

Lee has some interesting overall conclusions that can also help traders become more like a shark:

- Only invest in your best ideas.

- Invest a decent amount in each idea.

- Be greedy when winning – embrace the possibility of winning big.

- Adapt when you are losing: have a plan and stick to it.

- Only invest in liquid stocks.

Bears vs tribesmen

Now comes a BUT.

The only thing I would warn about being a Connoisseur is that they did brilliantly in a bull market. What about if a bear market hits and shares keep going down?

It is possible all these characters could lose in a down market of a year or two, even the Connoisseurs.

When a bear market strikes, I would argue that the Connoisseurs must think about a reversal of strategy and consider shorting. At that point, the psychological characteristics of a Connoisseur might run into problems.

It should be different for shark traders as we discussed in chapter 4.

While I think all of Lee's fund managers would come to him and report losses in a bear market, at the very worst I think sharks could report break-even – maybe even a profit!

The broker's view

I asked Connor Campbell, financial analyst at Spreadex (some of the people who actually take people's trades), what makes a psychologically successful trader from his insider's viewpoint.

Here's his take on it:

Winning traits of traders

- "Stoicism in the face of a painful day of trading, a stiff upper lip when the chips are down."

- "Being prepared to cut losses. Sticking with an instrument because you 'just have a gut feeling about it' may work out some of the time, but more often than not if it looks like a donkey, and sounds like a donkey, then, my friend, you have a donkey."

- "Knowing why you are buying or selling. Those investors who put the time and effort into carefully selecting their portfolio have the mental fortitude to know when and when not to stand by their decisions."

- "Patience. Trading can require a steely-eyed resolve across the weeks and months, allowing a stock to right its upwards (or downwards) course amidst macro-inspired movements. Those looking for quick results, and even quicker profits, may be left wanting; those, however, that can withstand the pressure to interfere, those who have the mental strength to trust the decisions they have (hopefully) carefully made, are likely going to be the ones who end up with the biggest windfall."

- "Not meddling. Of course checking the day-to-day fluctuations of one's trades can be tempting, but for the investor's sanity, and success, the willpower to resist this impulse is vital. That doesn't mean ignoring, and failing to react to, red flags, but rather knowing when and when not to meddle. Obviously there are daily profits to be made (especially with short-selling), but for those traders aiming for long-term profits it is probably best that they have the self-control not to smear their sticky fingers all over their portfolio on a regular basis."

- "Poise. Even in irrational, volatile times, cool heads and calm decisions can lead to a green bit of land in a sea of choppy red waters. Matching the market's own volatility with panic, on the other hand, is a recipe for disaster, one that can undo even the most seasoned trader in a blink of an eye. It can be hard to keep composed when the world seems to be falling around your ears (a situation that can happen far more than one would like); those who have the sangfroid not to falter in the most trying of circumstances, the toughness to continue regardless, are those who can stand the heat of the calamity-filled kitchen we call the stock market."

- "Precision. Abandoning what you know (be that your fundamentals or your technicals, that is the trader's prerogative) can lead to ruinous results; as too can an unwillingness to change, a stubborn belief that you are right in the face of plunging charts and violently waving red flags. You won't get it right all the time; no one can. But such a constitution will help you be on the green side of the loss/gain divide more often than you aren't."

"Calamity filled kitchen" is a good description of the market. I also often think of the market as a drunk guy walking down the street. It's not really possible to decide which way he is going to go next – he doesn't know himself. Successful traders try and wait to see where the drunk guy might end his walk for a bit before deciding on some action.

"The ability to subordinate an impulse to a value is the essence of the proactive person. Reactive people are driven by feelings, by circumstances, by conditions, by their environment. Proactive people are driven by values – carefully thought about, selected and internalized values."

Stephen Covey

Let's now look in more depth at the various emotions that can play havoc with trading and what we can do to suppress them. The first thing we have to look at are those emotions that ignite our gambling instinct – starting with a desire for thrills, spills and excitement.

PART II:
The Eight Deadly Emotions

"Success in investing doesn't correlate with I.Q. once you're above the level of 125. Once you have ordinary intelligence, what you need is the temperament to control the urges that get other people into trouble in investing."

Warren Buffett

Excitement

I suspect practically everyone who decides to trade has a gambling streak somewhere inside them. I definitely do. I actually started work in a bookies the moment I turned 18. I loved the thrill of the horses and played the fruit machines in my lunch break.

I even became a full-time horse gambler for a couple of years but could never make that much out of it, even with inside info at times. So yes, I *definitely* have a gambler inside me. But that's bad news if you want to make money from trading. The need for thrills and spills – plain old excitement – can be fatal.

"Psychological research suggests that some individuals are more impulsive than others and less conscientious about adhering to plans and intentions. These personality traits often are accompanied by stimulation seeking and a high degree of risk tolerance: a deadly combination."

Brett Steenbarger

How and why exactly does it mess up traders – and what can be done about it? Let's take a look.

How it affects traders

Some people are *gambaholics*. Gambling addiction, like alcohol addiction, is an illness – it will always try to conquer you and the only way to control it is never to gamble. If you're a gambaholic, please don't try trading – or quit now if you've already started.

But I reckon a less severe gambling instinct is very common among traders. Think of it as a need for a bit of a 'fix', something akin to taking a drug, a need for excitement. Just 'taking a punt' on a share for the hell of it without doing any research. Buying a share using any excuse – a mate told you or someone on a bulletin board said you could fill your boots.

It is extremely hard to expunge gambling from your brain. The lure of punts is very addictive. Traders love the idea of buying a small oil company and making a million from a tiny initial investment. After oil companies, it's any company with a cure for cancer just around the corner. Or a penny share. Anything where there is a huge risk.

Rob's tale

A desire for excitement can lead to big losses very quickly. Here is Rob's story:

> "I managed to lose roughly £20,000 in the course of a few days. When you said to beware of trading the indices, I decided I knew better, and the string of winning trades on the FTSE I enjoyed over the next three months only convinced me further that I possessed a rare talent.

> "I took out various shorts on the Dow and FTSE, losing all contact with sanity – convinced of a correction – then I woke up to find all my positions had been margin-called overnight as

futures had risen, giving me huge losses and taking most of my starting capital."

Rob told me this story in person. He knew that he had fallen into a gambling trap for the sake of excitement. He admitted he had started to get hooked on watching the indices go up and down continually. He said he couldn't resist. Of course, the worst thing is that Rob started off by winning. It meant he thought he knew better even when things turned against him.

Rob was keen to give up gambling on trading indices and had come to a seminar to put this right and concentrate on 'proper' investing. He contributed well during the day and I thought he was going to succeed as a trader now that he had quit the gambling habit.

Two months later he came to a follow-up seminar. He's a lovely guy and I was pleased to see him. He said he was doing fine on the investment front. But he had started gambling on the indices again!

I expressed some doubt about him as a trader. He had part of a shark's approach when it came to investing. And with his betting he could even see what was the right thing to do. He set stop-losses on his bets to try and make sure he didn't lose too much. He was trying to take the emotion out of it – but indices move up and down too much. Stop-losses just get taken out. You lose too often.

One morning he said he had woken up to find all his positions had been taken out and he had lost another few thousand. He had come to the follow-up event to try and get back on the straight and narrow.

He agreed with my reservations and said he wasn't sure he could stop. I think I knew the reason why: again, emotion. He had lost so much to the market. Now, rather than worry about a longer-term profit, he wanted to win back what he had lost. He wanted revenge. As we'll cover in the next chapter, this is just another way a trader gets lured into ever more gambling.

There was only one way to change: cut the gambling completely. Take indices off his screens. Only ever look at shares.

I lost touch with him after this. I fear the gambler's need for excitement was too strong for him.

Tim's tale

Tim is another trader who went astray in the search for excitement:

> "My first spread bet was on August 24th. I saw the FTSE Index going to hell fast and wanted some of the action. I quickly got an account set up but it took too long. Then I dived in without looking at the chart again and made a horrible fat finger trade mistake by hitting the USA 500 rolling instead of the FTSE 100 rolling right at the moment when the DOW opened with a 1000 point loss and started racing north.
>
> "I lost €1,500 in ten minutes. I would have lost it trading the FTSE anyway because I got in at the lowest point it has been at, but it would have moved much slower and I might have understood how to exit... Also I bought a bunch of illiquid shares and I held onto a share after I was 110% in profit, because I listened to all the screaming on the bulletin boards..."

Here is more mad gambling in the pursuit of excitement – he wasn't trying to calmly hedge his portfolio with a short. He wanted "some of the action", just like he got excited by the "screaming on the bulletin boards".

How to fix gambling for excitement

It is a tough ask to *totally* zap the gambling impulse from your brain. For gambaholics, completely avoiding it is the only answer – even a little bit of gambling is soon fatal. For others, there is a less drastic answer.

Firstly, you have to admit there is a gambler in you looking for excitement and that it will come out at some point – maybe on a boring day. And it has the potential to destroy you if it takes hold. Keeping that awareness is important.

Secondly, open a separate gambling account.

Take 5% of your trading pot. Or 10% tops if you really must. Open a completely separate account. And I really do mean separate. It's no good just doing this in your ISA and trusting yourself to keep track of the spending.

 Don't use a spread betting account for this. With spread betting you can lose more than your initial investment. The worst a share can do is go to zero.

Gamble as much as you like within this account. Yes, really *gamble*. Buy all the crap you want. Small oil shares, companies with an upcoming cure for cancer. Tiny illiquid shares. Don't bother with research; try to catch falling knives; follow any bad behaviour your heart desires...

Indeed, use your heart. Use your emotions! Gamble! Do *not* be a shark with it in any way. This is what I do and it really works. I just use 5% of my entire capital to gamble.

You'll find that this will give you all the excitement you crave.

Just remember: use a totally separate account. An example: you have a £50,000 pot. (By pot I mean the total you have in shares and cash that you have set aside for investing or trading.) Take £2,500 or maybe £5,000 of it and put that in a totally different account – preferably with a different broker. Play with that money and enjoy the gambling. Once you've lost some of it, only add in more if your primary money has risen significantly through investing elsewhere. Don't be an idiot and blow the 5% and come back for another 5% six months later and another 5% six months after that.

And whatever you do, always, *always* limit it to a small per cent of your total pot.

If you have been finding yourself gambling for excitement, wanting that rush of adrenaline, try this idea. See if it works. You are Captain Kirk in your small gambling account and Mr Spock in your main account. You get all the thrills and spills you want without ending up sleeping in shop doorways.

Desperation

Unfortunately, it's not just a lust for thrills and spills that drives traders to gamble. There's another motivation: desperation.

The gambling rush of the previous chapter – how do you know you are in it? The key signs are: making lots of trades, a feeling of excitement, shouting, jumping up and down, sweaty palms, an out-of-control feeling and a 'Who cares?' attitude.

The gambling you'll see in this chapter manifests itself with the key signs of: holding your head in your hands, shaking, wishing you had never been born.

What's strange is that some traders can start off like sharks, but then the gambling instinct suddenly rears its head. When that happens you must recognise it fast. It's usually desperation that's driving it, often after a sudden flare of excitement drove you into it.

Steve's tale

Steve came to a couple of my seminars and I knew he was doing well as he would email me occasionally, sounding quite happy. He was a great guy – and ironically, since we have been talking about Vulcans in this book, a sci-fi buff. So he knew what it meant to stay Mr Spock and not turn into Captain Kirk.

I thought Steve would carry on doing fine, maybe not setting the trading world on fire – but making steady money over the years. And then… this email arrived in my inbox:

> "I've not had a bad run recently on longs and shorts. I've been making real money and progress, following the charts and flows of the market. But then I decided to invest in a share because it looked cheap. It fell with the China news, but instead of selling I hung on and averaged down too.

> "Monday I felt the floor fall away when the markets opened. My positions were closed by the spread betting company, any profit is gone and now I'm in debt.

> "I've never felt so stupid. I have to write or call them with a heavy heart to find out how to pay them. I should never have relied on margin."

I knew right away what he'd done. Initially, the first form of gambling (**'Give me excitement now!' gambling**) had reared its head. The market had become volatile and, with the low oil price, commodity stocks were falling – among them a FTSE 100 giant, Glencore.

Steve had decided to stop being unemotional and transformed himself into Captain Kirk. Instead of enjoying the slow steady rises he thought, let's give it a go – this is a massive company, it is going to bounce hard and fast so I'll be in the money!

He bought mega amounts using the leverage the spread betting firm allowed him. Steve was now gambling with someone else's money, leaving himself open to emotions flooding in. As the shares continued to retreat, his losses grew, and the second form of gambling reared its head (**'Oh God please no!' gambling**).

Steve bought more and more shares, got more and more emotional, became increasingly convinced the shares would bounce and he'd get a big payout.

It didn't happen. He ran out of credit with the spread bet firm which – as it was entitled to – closed out all his positions and sent him a bill. Payable immediately. Steve went into denial and kind of blamed the firm. How could they expect him to pay immediately? It was all their fault for giving him the credit. Anyway he can't pay them the full amount.

I suggested he offer to pay them in monthly instalments, otherwise they could issue a summons and it wouldn't be long before the bailiffs were round. Soon after this I received my last email from Steve:

> "I've taken myself out of the share market. Since we last corresponded I've started to pay the spread bet firm a monthly sum but this has not been easy on the pocket, nor has dealing with them – it ended up rather heated.

> "A word of warning to your readers would be: don't dabble with what you can't afford to lose and never be tempted to rely on margin. I'm sure you've said that many times before.

> "On reflection I can see a few more errors I made. The biggest one was trading in my current situation. I am the only earner due to family illness and was trying to make fast money to subsidise monthly income.

> "I don't drink, smoke or go out that much and rarely buy any luxury goods for myself, so all cash goes on the essentials in life (mortgage, bills, car, food).

"So the risk was silly, made me desperate and has left me on a knife edge. The only good thing to come out of this is looking for a better paid job and I may have an offer on the table next week. Life is an experience, I'm sure I will learn from this."

If Steve had been cold and logical he would have realised he simply did not have enough money to 'play the markets'. Unemotionally, looking at the cards life was dealing him, he should have been out of the market completely. In effect he had no money to run 'the business'.

If Steve was a shop he was doing the equivalent of buying stock on a credit card when he couldn't afford to pay the card back.

When things went against him, it was inevitable that he got desperate and started gambling. You simply cannot be in the market at all in this state. It is the same as trying to pay your gas bill by going to the bookies and sticking cash on a horse. If you don't have money you can afford to lose, wait till you have. And then don't borrow to put more on. There is no such thing as a reliable way to make fast money, only fast losses.

The fact that Steve felt a little angry, almost blaming the spread bet firm for asking for its money, means he definitely did the right thing in quitting the markets for now. Let's face it, Steve would have been rather angry if he'd won and the spread bet firm said it couldn't pay him. As Yoda almost said, losses lead to anger, anger leads to hate, hate leads to suffering in the form of a 25-stone man turning up outside your front door at five o'clock in the morning to take your television and your children's beds away in his van.

Rob's tale

Another tale of **'Give me excitement now!' gambling** turning into **'Oh God please no!' gambling** comes from another Rob:

"I've read your spread betting book and trading book and had some success last year. However, for some reason this year I started with more money, figuring I would ride the Santa rally and earnings season with a bigger bet on FTSE 100.

"Anyway, it's all gone very wrong and I was hoping you could put me onto anyone for advice or an outside look at the situation I'm in. Are you sitting down? I basically rode down the crash from new year and panicked and shorted at the market bottom with no stop-loss!

"I'm not sleeping. I may have to close all or go mad. I can't pluck up courage to take action.

"My plan at the mo is to close the buy at the end of this rally, maybe today or Monday, then hope sentiment drops and I can recoup some middle ground in the next dip.

"The spread bet firm recommended I close everything as I sounded erratic on the phone. They have frozen my account and will only let me close positions and move limits – no more bets. I want to minimise damage but like I said I am too scared to take action as I'm up against the wall on losses.

"PS. I know you can't take a stance but have we bottomed? Bear or bull! I was bull all the way till the 20th, now bear, but this talk of oil deals and production cutbacks is amplifying.

"PPS. Do you know any shrinks I can talk to!"

I felt terribly sorry for Rob. He was obviously in a bad state psychologically and light years away from being a shark. Even the spread betting firm, to its credit, recognised he was in trouble and stopped him being able to do any more trades.

When someone is in this condition there is only one answer: a total halt, everything must be closed out and preferably the account then closed. The bill paid, never to venture into trading again, unless – just possibly – whatever in his life that was causing the bad behaviour ceases.

He probably doesn't want me to say, "Shut everything down". He'd like me to say, "Carry on, you just went through a bad patch, it will all be OK. It will roll back in your favour..." With his last line he even asks me my opinion on which way the market is going to go!

There was only one thing for it: send him a strongly worded email. The good thing is, I think it did the trick. He told me he asked the firm to stop everything and end it. I hope that was true.

A terrible shame

Excitement, then, is often a gateway to desperation and an even more dangerous form of gambling.

But I'm afraid there is also a third circle of gambling Hell. It's just next door to desperation so we'll cover it in this chapter. It's even harder to get out of. It's shame-trading.

Once a trader has been beaten down and ruined his or her account, there can be a temptation to keep going even when there is no money – after all, it would be awful to give in now. And there's always friends and family to borrow from. Of course, you won't tell them why you need the money exactly (that would be embarrassing), and you certainly won't tell them why you can't pay them back when you lose it (that would be mortifying).

If you're very unlucky, after losing the first lot they lend you they will agree to lend you even more money when you come back to them.

Shame sets incredibly powerful traps. It can send traders into a death spiral. By and large I am optimistic about everyone's ability to become more like a shark or Mr Spock. But if you have ever fallen into this pattern of trading, or think it remotely likely that you might, I'm afraid the only way to live long and prosper is to delete your trading account. Trading isn't worth destroying yourself and others over.

On this topic, here is an interesting contribution from a reader of mine called Victoria:

> "Fear and greed are written about a lot in trading books but there seems a real lack of anyone looking into that most toxic of human emotions – shame.

> "No one seems to want to go there. But it seems to me, especially after reading some of the awful tales of people losing houses, relationships, pretty much everything, that when all the fear and greed impulses have died away and the beaten up trader staggers off the rollercoaster and surveys the carnage of their trading account, shame rears its ugly head.

> "This can go on to drive more destructive tendencies– aggression, blaming others, more out-of-control trading or withdrawal, not just from trading but from family, friends and ultimately sometimes the world. There is no stronger argument for good discipline and money management than reflecting on the damage that can be inflicted by out-of-control trading.

"Fear and greed are often portrayed as two separate impulses but they are more interlinked than might at first appear. What looks like bargain-hunting greed can actually be driven by a fear impulse. That's what averaging down is all about. And taking profits too early – it's that fear of losing it all as well as wanting to have it right now."

Some of the things Victoria discusses there are pretty bleak. If you ever feel yourself going down this road it probably means other stuff in your life isn't right and the only thing to do is to stop trading forever and go to Gamblers Anonymous for help and understanding.

Greed

Greed for traders usually takes the form of thinking about making a lot of money really quickly. The tell-tale signs are pound signs appearing on your eyeballs. Keep a mirror handy.

Greed is the downfall of many. It's such a common emotion. We can't help it – we're a selfish animal. We want to make money quickly and lots of it. And this is where Sod's Law comes into it:

The more money we try to make and the quicker we try to make it, the less likely it is to happen.

There are lots of different types of greed in the market. I am going to tackle the main two because they crop up most often and do the most damage.

1. The lure of the long shot

The first form of greed is the lure of the long shot. One trade to change everything! It usually makes traders buy a tiny share in the hope it springs higher and makes them pots and pots of money.

Barry's tale

This brings me to Barry. He told me he had a very decent pot of £200,000 to try and make money with in the markets.

If he traded like a shark or Mr Spock he would have gone down the focused/logical route of trying to find 20 or so good companies for his portfolio and aiming to get 10–25% on his money over a year or so, turning it into £220,000–£250,000.

Instead he got greedy: he stuck the full £200,000 into a tiny share called Coms at 12p. He could think of little else but Coms going to 60p. It would make him a millionaire.

No shark would do this. Mr Spock wouldn't either. It makes no sense to put all your money in a single tiny penny share:

- The share could go to 50p. It could also go to 5p. Or 0p. Small firms do from time to time. How do you trade your way out of that?

- Even if the share went to 50p, penny shares are notoriously illiquid. In other words, there aren't necessarily enough people willing to buy shares in the market at the highest price the market is quoting. He might only have been able to sell £10,000 of shares at 50p.

Not such a cunning plan after all, eh?

The role of greed in his trade was immediately obvious. There was nothing logical about, "If this share gets to 50p I will be a millionaire!" The 'If' there contains as much logic as a chocolate teapot. (Crikey, is that the time, we're in chapter 8 and I've not a cuppa in ages. One sec…)

He probably thought – '50p isn't so much more than 10p. It couldn't take much to go up to that.'

Well, maybe it's not a big difference when you're looking at the loose change in your pocket. *But it is an increase of 500%.* How many shares go up by 500%? How much of anything in life goes up by 500%? (You wish yours did!)

Barry was sure the market for the share was about to boom, fuelled by the bulletin board where everyone was telling him to buy in quick. It went down 30%. He didn't change his mind.

He did go a bit white when I suggested that, because it was such a small share, it might be impossible to sell much even at 7p. He hadn't realised it can be hard to sell small illiquid shares.

As it happened, the 7p quoted really was only good for a small amount. I said that if it was me I would start shifting some every day to raise cash to put into something else. Hell, I even said I would press the button for him.

He didn't take me up on the offer. I don't think anything I could say would make him sell.

The shares went to a penny three months later. I am pretty certain he never sold. That was the end of his career in the stock market. Nearly all his money gone – and all because of greed.

Jerry's tale

Jerry's is a more positive story. He's a trader who managed to transform himself from a cocky Captain Kirk lured by the long shot into the twin of Mr Spock.

I remember Jerry very well. He was a nice guy, into surfing and stuff like that. He lived in Thailand and wasn't much bothered by material things. He just wanted to be able to fund a reasonable lifestyle.

But he had got greedy.

He'd bought one share called JQW, purchasing £11,000 of stocks at an average of 50p per share. By the time I was talking to him it stood at 9p. He had lost a great deal of money on it, on paper at any rate.

Now he was struggling in his mind whether to dump it and take the loss. He was convinced the share was going to go back up and gave me the usual speech on how it wasn't worth selling now.

But he listened to what I had to say ("Sell, you muppet!"). He sold those shares that very day. The next week they went up a little – oh dear, I thought, here we go; the firm will probably be bid for and he'll hate me forever.

But JQW went bust. Jerry would have lost the whole lot. He saved quite a bit of money.

And – even better – he had become a shark. In the weeks following he told me things had changed. He was practising total discipline, using stops – things were going well. He had adopted to the ways of Spock with remarkable ease. I think it might be that his brain was already pretty uncluttered – he practised meditation.

He promised me that would he never again keep a losing stock. He explained:

> "I learnt to not pay so much attention to the stated fundamentals but instead to think about why a share price is tanking despite strong fundamentals."

Which is exactly right – you can believe there are strong fundamentals, but if a share price is going down *sharply* there is probably a reason. You may not be aware of what it is. But it doesn't matter. You quit before losing lots of money. You live to fight another day.

2. I am a god

Financial analyst and trader Connor Campbell sees what goes on in thousands of trades every day at Spreadex. Earlier he shared what he has seen makes for a successful trader. We also talked about what the biggest danger is for traders – interestingly, in his view, it's greed.

In particular, the second form of greed. The kind that makes traders go round thinking: "I am a god." (Shortly before the markets comprehensively disprove their religion.)

"There is a lot of greed about," said Connor. "It might seem an odd thing to lambast a trader over. In the immortal – if out-of-context – words of Gordon Gekko, *greed is good.*

"But nothing is more dangerous than a trader who over-extends himself because his head has grown a little too big after only a few profitable trades. People susceptible to a rapidly expanding ego at the slightest signs of success quickly come unstuck. It's a trait that leads people to make more and more rash decisions based on nothing more than hubris."

Alpesh's tale

Here is a story from a reader called Alpesh. He explains how the second kind of greed undid him.

"After a successful 2014 I thought I was a stock market genius and went in big in 2015. My average position size was around £6,000 in 2014. But in 2015, feeling confident, I took a large positions in a handful of stocks. This included £100,000 in ETO, £40,000 in JLG, £60,000 in TEF, £30,000 in QP. and £30,000 in CINE. In total I had a portfolio of roughly £250,000 – almost all of it borrowed. I was doing well. I had a paper profit of £30,000 after a few months and I was once again feeling like the king of stocks.

"Then it started to fall apart. ETO kept sinking. The rest came down slowly every week. Soon I was in loss. But instead of taking a quick 10% loss like I used to do, I couldn't face it when it meant losing so much money.

"With a £100,000 position, even an 8% loss was £8,000! I froze. How could I have been up and now down? So I kept all the positions open despite being down at least £2,000 in all of them apart from CINE. With QP. I had been up 20% at one point but now found myself down 15% and unable to unwind such a large position on a small stock with a wide spread.

"Then came August 2015 and the market went into meltdown. My margin was thin so I panicked and sold out at the worst point at a large loss. Overall I was down almost 12%, which wasn't much compared to the percentage gains made in previous years – but having such large positions meant that I was down £27,000.

"After taking such a large loss I have decided to take some time out of the market and start slow again. I guess my advice to anyone is do not increase your position size until your account is very, very large and always have stops in the market to avoid emotional problems."

At least Alpesh realised he needed to take himself out of the market and that greed had caused him severe problems.

James' tale

Sometimes greed can even hit someone who starts off trading as cool and emotionless as you can imagine. Those qualities bring success. And success means even the most sober trader can start feeling like some sort of trading deity about to sweep all before them.

When James had only recently started trading he came to a seminar of mine and noticed I bought a share during the seminar that he really liked too. He went away and bought lots more of it. Some time later, the share was bid for – and he sent me a message of deep joy. We had both made substantial sums on it – I think he made more than £150,000.

Like me, he had managed to hold it for several years, from around 150p to a tenner – so we multi-bagged on it, as the awful stock market phrase goes. (It just means when something more than doubles in price. It has nothing to do with when you manage to steal two Tesco Bags for Life while the girl on the till isn't looking.)

I was very impressed he had had the patience to hold on. I assumed he was probably a true cold-blooded shark. I was very pleased indeed.

But I didn't hear from him after that. I wondered how he was getting on but I had lost his email address. I remembered his nickname on the bulletin boards, so in a fit of curiosity one day I did a search.

Sadly, I found out he wasn't a shark after all. After making so much money, instead of using that cash to fund a new portfolio following some simple tried-and-tested rules, he put the lot into a risky oil stock... which went bust, taking all the money he had been so patient in building up. He had succumbed to the second form of greed.

Here's what he said after he bought the new share with the money he had so painstakingly made:

> "Putting this out there... I'm honestly chuffed to bits to be picking this oil co up at these prices. It may come back to haunt me but I doubt it. Crude low + CEO dodgy deals now sacked off, perfect storm. Way oversold says I, 150p this year doubles my money."

After purchasing the shares, the share price started a big slide. Did he set a stop-loss and get out? No, because immortal, invincible, share-trading gods do not use stop-losses. He did seem a bit miffed not to have much money lying around to double-down on his godlike decision, however:

"Obviously today's share price is dire, however even with low crude prices next year, it's looking like it is about to have a great 2015 in relation to sucking the black stuff out the ground. Anything under 80p is a bargain it seems, I'm all in but I wish I had another 50K spare."

A shark wouldn't have got into this trade at all, but if somehow he did his next post would have been very different to the above. It would simply have said:

"I am an idiot for allowing this trade in my account at all, but because I am a shark I gave it what I give all my trades: a stop-loss. The share just hit it. I am out. It was a bad buy but an unemotional sell."

Tellingly, James used the poker player's term "all in" – it sounds like he needs to read chapters 6 and 7 too. It was actually just as well he hadn't got another £50,000 spare. After this, the share fell further.

Then, eventually, it stopped falling. There was even a small rise. James said:

"I'm guessing this recent upward trend is the build up to an announcement. Things are looking a lot rosier…"

All is not lost (no James, of course not, just a hundred grand!). He gets a little lift from others who are also hopeful. Then… the shares are suspended. After that, they are de-listed.

The shareholders lose everything.

His final post reads as follows:

"After reading news of directors lining their own pockets, I assumed it was just oversold. A couple of new faces would soon take the heat off. Since then Mr Brent decided to go AWOL and a previously bursting oil find dried up overnight. I accept my buy was a massive risk and accept where I am today because of my decisions. I could have bought a new Ferrari with my initial investment, but it's the bus now lol. I'm fortunate to make my own cash during the week and have a few properties to fall back on, others whom I assume are retired may not be so lucky. Without sounding like a knob, I've never 'had' use of the money and can carry on regardless without it, albeit with my tail betwixt my legs."

I am so glad he didn't lose his house or anything on this terrible, terrible trade. I remember having a drink with him after that seminar years ago; he was great. And hopefully if he ever goes back in the markets again he has learned from his mistakes. He let greed get the better of him. Not the grasping kind of greed you might think of when you hear that term – but the subtle, refined and considerably more expensive greed of someone who thinks successful trades have given him a seat on Mount Olympus.

The fact that he thought of his trading pot in terms of "a new Ferrari" is the giveaway in that last post. He also blamed the oil price among other things instead of blaming himself. That's not a good sign. But it's positive that he does accept it was his decisions that were to blame – and he has also wisely invested in property so he is not exactly going to be begging on the streets. He played with money he could afford to lose. But, I don't know about you, but I am never prepared to lose £150,000, even I can afford to.

Interestingly another poster replied to James on his bulletin board (before the share was de-listed):

> "Glad you posted, it's always comforting to know others had the same thoughts and are now in the same boat. I could have bought myself a nice house here in Cape Town with my 'investment'. I'm hoping it might recover enough to at least buy me a little apartment sometime in the far-distant future!"

This poster believed there was still some chance of recovery! It just goes to show: when you buy a share, your thoughts should never turn to the material things you think you might be able to buy with the proceeds.

Keep those thoughts totally separate.

James' story goes to show: even if one element can go right (the patience to get the big payout on one share) another element can go wrong (not selling when it didn't go right the next time) if you let emotions get the better of you.

"Trade like you don't need the money. It takes so much pressure off you."
Martin Niemi

The lure of leverage

One of the reasons a lot of people get too greedy is that it is so easy to borrow money to trade with – something a shark would never even consider.

In the old days of share trading no one would have dreamed of trading or investing with money they didn't have. But more recently, hundreds of firms have emerged that will allow you to trade a lot on a little.

I'm amazed that someone with no trading experience could be allowed to trade £20,000 worth of shares by stumping up just £2,000.

Borrowing/debt in general is why economies are in so much trouble around the world. We are all encouraged to take out as much debt as possible as it is in the providers' interest for us to do so. We have an "I want it now" society – and if I can't afford it, I'll just use a credit card to get it.

In my parents' generation you got paid cash for your work, you then paid for stuff from the cash – if you couldn't afford it you didn't buy it and hardly anyone was in debt.

The current generation is encouraged on all sides to take on more and more debt. New contactless cards make it even worse as you can now pay for a Starbucks with the flick of a wrist or a smartphone.

A shark would not dream of over-leveraging and realises the market can be crazy. Tight discipline is needed and borrowing to trade is the road to the poorhouse.

A shark would *maybe* leverage a little bit – but only a small amount in proportion to his or her funds, and never anything the shark can't afford to lose. You have to drum this boring phrase into the brain: **Do not play with money you cannot afford to lose.**

I have heard some trainers at seminars encourage their delegates to take money out on their credit cards to play with. Unbelievable!

Keep the debt in check, and you'll go a long way to keeping greed in check too.

Fear

Fear, like greed, is an emotion that sharks don't have any time for. Fear sells newspapers and magazines. Armageddon *really* shifts the copies.

We are scared we might end up with nothing. Or there will be a big war. Or terrorism will strike again. The fear of all these things is bigger than any reality. Most people think wars kill more people than murders, which they believe kills more people than suicides. Wrong! Of the three, suicide is the biggest killer, then murder, then war.

We're scared of flying – but one plane has passed over where I live every minute for 50 years and *not one* has crashed on its way into Heathrow. I am scared of turbulence even though, being a fan of *Air Crash Investigation*, I know it's like a car going over a minor bump in the road and nothing is going to happen to me.

In 1999 there was a fear that all computers would go down because they couldn't cope with the year 2000.

Same with shares. When they are going down there is an insane fear they will all go to zero. The risk of something we fear is usually pretty small.

Most traders suffer unnecessary fear. As Mark Douglas points out, there is the fear of being wrong, fear of missing out, fear of losing and the fear of leaving money on the table (usually fivers and 50ps in my case):

> "I found that basically, those four fears accounted for probably 90% to 95% of the trading errors that we make. Let's put it this way: If you can recognize opportunity, what's going to prevent you from executing your trades properly? Your fear. Your fears immobilize you. Your fears distort your perception of market information in ways that don't allow you to utilize what you know."

In my experience it is rare for one of the fears to operate in isolation. They're all natural allies and can push and pull you in different directions at different times.

Here is an example of fear in action:

Eric's tale

Eric came to a follow-up seminar where I'd asked everyone to bring a share with them for us to study.

The price of Eric's share at the time was 21p. Eric told us how fabulous a buy it was, how lowly rated, how many brilliant businesses it had…

I asked him if he had already bought it. Yes, he had – at 27p. So he was already down nearly 25% on his original buy.

"But why are you still in it?" I asked. He had been to previous seminars and we had talked endlessly about getting out of shares that go wrong. He must have known you should be out well before 25% losses.

"I don't know," said Eric. "I just didn't. But now I am scared of missing out if it goes back up."

I checked supply and demand on the share – it didn't look good. I had to tell Eric that if it was me I would get out fast and come back when it might well be lower still. Better to take the hit and move on. Mr Spock would have cut this at 25p for a 5% loss and that's what he should have done.

Happily, Eric set phasers to kill like a top graduate from Starfleet Academy.

He immediately sold, took the loss and lived to fight another day. And on top of that he told me it would never happen again. He could see that it had been fear – most of all of missing out on a recovery (with elements of the other three fears in the background) – that had left him trapped with a share that showed no logical signs of outperforming any time soon.

Conquering fear

Fear leads to some terrible losses – makes us sell at the wrong time, buy at the wrong time; sell because everyone else is selling, buy because everyone is buying. As Warren Buffett once said, the best time to buy is when everyone is fearful. Another investing legend, Sir John Templeton, liked to wait to buy a company until it hit the "point of maximum pessimism". That's the way to do it!

If you are about to press the sell button in fear, the chances are you should be switching to the buy button instead. Fear also stops people from running profits – "better bank the small profit in case it goes down and I lose it".

What can you do to conquer fear in your trading and make sure you stick to your trading plan like Mr Spock?

When I feel fear trying to make me deviate from my plans, I don't do anything complicated. I just get off the computer and go and do something – anything – else. Even if it is to load the dishwasher. (Though I don't get to do that anymore as I am told you have to wash the dishes before they go in these days.) That clears my head. It helps me trust the wisdom of my plan and only take actions that I know to be logical.

I know that for some people that might not be enough. They want more reassurance. I get that, though whatever in the markets is causing the fear won't go away overnight – so the best you can do is find a way to live with it without trading self-destructively. A reader of mine called Fiona wrote to me recently with some great info on how she overcomes fear and finds reassurance she can trust. I am pretty sure she is a true shark.

Fiona's fear-killing plan

"As I write this, the overwhelming feeling in the markets is fear. The useful little table on the page I use to research stocks is telling me that only 4% of stocks are up on the day, compared with 39% declining and 57% unchanged. That tells me that most people are either out of the market or sitting waiting, a load more are still selling, and a very small amount got lucky. At least I am not alone.

"After weeks of China and oil we have gone through the initial 'Everything's down so let's buy' into a world of enduring pain. It's now a test of stamina. It would be very easy to snap all of a sudden and sell everything – you can feel the panic in the wings. You can't let fear get the upper hand but you do have to accommodate it somehow – simply ignoring it is not the way to go.

"This is what I do to stay sane:

"**Get reading.** I dig out some of my old favourite trading books: (Shameful plug for *The Naked Trader* deleted – Robbie.), *Come into My Trading Room* by Alexander Elder is another good one and I also like *The Little Book of Bull Moves in Bear Markets* by

Peter D. Schiff. This is about reminding myself that we are just in a cycle, the world is not ending today and helps bring my rational self back into play.

"**Step up physical activity.** Garden, gym, whatever. It is all about getting rid of excess adrenaline and directing nervous energy in the right place. Also it helps with the diet so at least one of my New Year resolutions remains intact.

"**Look at history.** It doesn't necessarily repeat itself but it does remind us of possibilities. Looking into what happened to value stocks after the last market crash is really very interesting and reminds me not to sell.

"**Prune.** I take a hatchet to my spread betting accounts. But I keep my shares. There will always be a cluster of spread bets that lose me money when the market has turned like this. I live with it.

"**Write.** It stops me freaking out and overtrading. Writing anything at all is a good idea. Three pages of A4 in longhand a day on anything you like will help calm down your subconscious and give you a fresh perspective. Try it – it works.

"**Don't talk yourself down.** We all have demons with their voices: "How much?", "You did what?", "You really are rubbish at this, aren't you?". Ignore them: they never help.

"**Plan.** I spend time drawing up a trading strategy for crap conditions. This includes position sizing, the sort of trades to avoid, a list of key dates and so on. It's a bit like an emergency plan and it makes me feel better. Some of it I end up using, some of it I don't. Just the process of pulling it together makes me feel a bit more in control, so look for reasonable, rational things to do like that. Above all be kind to yourself.

"**Turn the TV off.** Don't have the news channel on in the background. Everything becomes a crisis with a 24-hour newsfeed."

I think all of the above is excellent advice from Fiona – she has developed a strategy to deal with fear; you need to develop yours. Anything that can calm you down.

When fear is your friend

Can fear ever be your friend? A shark or Vulcan tries to cut out all emotions but… well, we're still always going to be human… and for some the next best thing might be being so aware of what it means that you're able to take action.

It's not for everyone, but it's an interesting angle on the emotion! A reader writes:

> "Most of the time I am a pretty calm trader but I have my emotional and mental blind spots and sometimes stay in a stock too long, usually a stock with a good story, until the damage has been done and everyone else is long gone. What I have noticed is that sometimes when I am trading I begin to feel anxious or want to avoid going through my portfolio for no apparent reason. Sometimes I wake at night feeling jittery. Cue fear.

> "I take this as an early warning sign that something is going wrong, perhaps one of my shares has weak price action which I have been glibly explaining away or perhaps I am just out of sync with the markets. It's a great emotional heads-up that I need to pay attention to something, especially as it happens before my thought processes have consciously registered I need to do something.

> "Likewise greed. Greed is my friend in that it gets me averaging up on really good shares. Ultimately that is how I make my decent money. But you kind of know when you're overdoing it – it's like having one chocolate bar too many and suddenly you can't stand the sight of Kit Kats. That's my cue to rein in.

"Not all feelings of fear and greed are the same and I have had to learn some discernment. There is a difference between a well-founded anxiety because I am getting something wrong and a slightly hysterical sensation of getting swept along with the herd's desire to sell everything because we're all doomed. How can I tell which is which? Well, strange as it sounds, they are slightly different sensations. If I am going with the herd, the feeling is panicky and in my head. If it is a problem with my own trading, it's more of a niggle that won't go away and it's in my gut. I take one as a cue to buy, the other as a cue to sell – so it is important to work out which is which.

"So there you have it. For me, fear and greed are my trading boundaries and they often appear seemingly from nowhere. Come up against either of them and I put on the brakes and think again."

Egomania

Ah, egomania. If you're one of the (probably) few women reading this book (most traders are men) pat yourself on the back – women suffer a lot less from this. A big ego is a major problem for traders and something a shark shouldn't even think of entertaining.

It's all fine and dandy to have an ego in other aspects of life. After all, most of the people who get to the top positions in their field have big egos. That drives them to succeed. But it's not much good in trading. That big ego stops you from taking losses. Makes you trade too much. Makes you do all sorts of silly things.

Here's a trader I met who had been brought low by his ego. (Except for his self-esteem, which was still flying as high as the USS Enterprise.)

Harry's tale

Harry came to a seminar of mine. Short of ripping off his shirt and zip-lining into his chair from a helicopter hovering outside the seminar room, he did everything possible to convey his status as an alpha male.

He actually asked a lot of questions but it soon became clear he wasn't listening to much that I was talking about. Hunched over an alpha male laptop, he was probably 'trading' while I was talking. He was, frankly, Mr Ego.

Everyone could tell he felt himself superior to the rest of the room – and superior to me – and I was supposed to be the teacher! He was just there to confirm what he was doing was right (and what I was doing was wrong).

The funny thing was, he was convinced he was right on everything… but he had lost a lot of money.

It was no surprise. I talked about a company on the day and why I thought I might buy it. I discussed my research. Harry piped up to say my research was wrong, as were my figures. I gently pointed out that my figures were right, taken directly from the company's report. He had got his from a website that hadn't updated to the latest figures. That's because he hadn't listened to the bit where I explained where to get the figures from.

If you let your ego sabotage your trading like Harry, don't be surprised when you run into problems. If he can't remove that emotion from his trading he hasn't got a chance of succeeding in the stock market.

Our ego is bound up with our pride and "achieving pride" is one of the "intangible motives" that psychologist Daniel Kahneman of Princeton University says really drives financial decision-making rather than money.

I don't want a desire to feel proud to affect my trading so I try not to brag to anyone when I have made a lot. But I have done it to the wife – and what's funny is I know when I am doing it. It's an alarm bell – every time I have bragged, it was time to bank profits.

A shark's solution

If you are to become a shark, the ego has to go. If you have got one, it won't be easy. Self-awareness doesn't come readily to someone with an ego.

I know, I know: 'Who the hell is this Robbie Burns to tell me I have an ego? Where does he get off suggesting I might be blind to my weaknesses? I could crush his head in one of my hands while putting on a successful Forex day-trade with my other and that's not even mentioning where I'd put my knee.'

Feeling like chucking this book out of the window now you've got to this chapter? Well, always make sure to open the window first – it can get expensive otherwise.

Also, maybe, just maybe, you have an ego.

Seriously, if something or someone is telling you that you might just have an ego… try and consider that possibility. *I* have an ego. I don't deny it. But when it comes to trading I ensure that it doesn't surface. I look at cold hard facts and if I get something wrong I admit it right away and cut the position.

Take a good hard look at yourself: do you think trading rules are for other people? Or you're simply a cut above others intellectually? Other people are a bit dim and you're the shining star? Nothing can go wrong for you?

Cut the ego to make money.

I find the best way to do this is to ring-fence your trading in your mind. However fantastic you think you are at everything – and however much better than anyone else – adopt the habit of thinking that in trading it's almost impossible to be Mr Perfect and that the rules really do apply to you as well as everyone else.

When things go wrong they are not suddenly going to right out of nowhere just because you are such an ace person. Say to yourself: 'Am I being a Kirk?' If so, think Spock.

Confirmation bias

A problem related to ego is called (Jargon claxon alert! – Ed.) *confirmation bias*.

What the hell is this?

Once you've got an idea in your head, it's hard not to look out for things that confirm it – whether it's that you believe someone doesn't like you or that you have a gambling system that really works. That's confirmation bias.

Sharks never have confirmation bias.

As a trader, confirmation bias could be, for example, when you really believe in a share or a decision you've made – and there is nothing anything or anyone can do to change your mind, even if perhaps in the back of your mind you realise you are wrong. And when you go and look for evidence to check whether you're right or wrong, you only zero in on the evidence that matches your conclusion.

It's only natural that confirmation bias afflicts most traders – even people well on the path to Vulcan naturalisation. When we buy a share we think we are making the right choice – that's why we bought it! And we made an effort. We did our research, we used a bit of technical analysis, we looked at the charts. We even waited to get our timing right. Some of you may have even looked at the Bollinger Band stochastics MACD crossover Elliottwavedeadcrossricepudding signals. (Hopefully not: as we'll cover in the next part of the book, your brain + bullshit = not good.)

The trouble is, once we have made up our mind and pressed the buy button – that is it. We are now 'in'! We expect the share price to rise because we are pretty good at stock picking, right? And once we are in, the next thing is to look around and make sure our choice is validated by others.

So it is off to the bulletin boards to check everyone else agrees the share is going up. And yah boo sucks to any moron who thinks differently. Anyone who thinks the share has got problems is a total (Censored. – Ed.). We're right. The charts say so. And the fundamentals. And the tipster bloke. And anyway there's going to be a bid next week! That bulletin board bloke knows his stuff.

Despite the share price continuing to go down, we will continue to scour the internet for more validation. Sell it? Are you crazy? Time to buy more! Look how cheap it is! It is just money lent! The markets always get things wrong. Mr Market is such a moron! Now it's got even cheaper – *great* news. Look at the price I can get it for now; it's like the sales. I'm in for *even more*.

You know what I'm getting at.

A shark's solution

What would a shark do instead of trying to get the validation that he or she is right about a share? A shark would do the opposite.

The easiest way to do this is to always think of alternative arguments when analysing shares you have bought or are about to buy.

OK, so we like a particular share. What we need to do is imagine looking at this share in six months' time. It has fallen 50%. Could it happen – and why? What if we are wrong? What if the oil it is supposed to have found turns out to be water – will it survive? Hang on, what about the debt? **Is whatever it makes easy to be copied? Could it be it won't get the licences it needs?** Perhaps it might not get approval for its biggest drug.

The one guy on the bulletin board who is spelling out the problems with the share, is it possible he is right and the rest of us... wrong?

Nowadays I tend to look for the negatives first. After all, this is a business and only the absolute best should get into my portfolio.

Confirmation bias is well-known in the aviation industry. The crash of Air France 447 in June 2009 had many contributing factors. But according to the final accident report, the copilot misinterpreted the aircraft's actual situation.

He was manually flying the aircraft because it had flown into icy conditions, causing some instruments to freeze up and the autopilot to fail. The speed indicator therefore incorrectly showed that the aircraft was flying too quickly, so he pulled the nose up – causing the stall warning system to activate for 54 seconds.

The pilots ignored the very loud warning alert because they didn't believe it to be correct – it did not fit with their picture of the world at that point. They believed the aircraft was flying too fast when in fact it was doing completely the opposite. As the aircraft continued to slow up, the noise from the stall warning system stopped because it wasn't designed to fly that slowly. So when the copilot pushed the nose of the aircraft down (which is the correct procedure to stop stalling) the aircraft accelerated and the warning returned. This supported his view that the aircraft was over speeding, so again he pulled the nose up – which exacerbated the stall, increased the rate of descent and proved fatal for 228 people.

Commercial pilots are trained in learning to recognise and minimise the adverse affects of confirmation bias. As a trader you should teach yourself to do the same.

When you are considering buying something, do not try and go looking for all the positives you can find. Look very carefully at all the negatives too. Try and find them and consider whether and how your buy could come unstuck.

Like pilots in the air, it might stop you buying shares that come crashing down to earth. (If you are flying somewhere shortly, have a great flight!)

Let's have a real-life example of confirmation bias.

Geoff's tale

I had just finished discussing confirmation bias at a seminar when Geoff in the front row showed us exactly how easy it is to have it, and how hard it can be to realise you have it.

I had been discussing confirmation bias with the group for a while. I then asked if anyone would like to share a general story, maybe about a trade that wasn't going well. Geoff said he had a lot of shares in a minerals company which produced potash. He admitted he had lost quite a lot on it so far. "It doesn't matter," he said cheerfully. "This one is going to be massive."

He then started telling us stories about all the permissions it was about to get, the orders that were about to come flying in and basically how amazing it was and how he couldn't understand why no one else in the room had bought shares in it.

Geoff obviously hadn't taken a real hard look at this share. He hadn't considered the risks and possible negatives at all. It just hadn't occurred to him. Even more unbelievably, he didn't seem to get that he had confirmation bias when I challenged him.

We had a look at the last results for the company.

"The problem is," I said, "it currently makes a big loss. It has £20m of cash left but it burned through half of that in the last year. Have you thought about what might happen if permissions get delayed and the cash runs out? There is a chance this could be down 50% at some point in the next year. If this was me I would be wary of it and make an unemotional business plan to get out quick if the share price begins to fall off a cliff."

Geoff wasn't having any of it. He said I hadn't got to grips with the amazing opportunities for the company and how he expected to make hundreds of thousands from it. I had to tell Geoff he had confirmation bias. No, he said, he didn't. But he did!

The next day I made a bet the shares would go down and indeed they halved over the next three months. I still hold my bet and I am in profit by £5,000. However, to ensure I didn't have 'negative' confirmation bias (like the more common positive variant, but this afflicts short sellers and Eeyore), I placed a stop-loss to get me out fairly fast if the shares start to rise.

My bet is Geoff still has those shares. And of course maybe he could still hit it lucky. But without confirmation bias he would have made a logical decision to have a stop-loss on the shares to get him out before too much damage was done and he wouldn't now be relying on enormous amounts of time and luck. **If he was still convinced by the share, he could now buy them back a lot lower.**

To recap, to avoid getting hit by confirmation bias:

- Every time you research a potential share, feel free to have a look at the good bits. (Profits are going up, the statement is strong, everything looks fine... You start reading bulletin boards and everyone says how amazing it is... Your heart starts to beat fast and you feel like you really want to press that buy button... The chart looks fab... Yes, let's buy! Buy! Buy!)

- Now press the reset button. Have a careful look at the previous few statements and search for negatives. One way is to look for negative words like 'challenging'. You could use the highlighter system from my book *The Naked Trader*. That picks out negative words from company releases in red. Is the share too good to be true? Hunt for the negative comments. Is the debt too big? One example of this in my own trading came when I was looking at a share called Aero Inventory. I was so keen on it. Everything was great: profits rising, a chart that showed I was getting in at a good time, it even had a nice dividend. But then I saw its profits were £33m while its debt was £450m! Way too much for me. It went bust a few months later. But how easy would it have been to buy it and only look at the positive and stick with it till it went bust? (Very, very easy.)

- Always use stop-losses when opening a trade.

Basically, accentuate the negative and eliminate the imbecilic... and you'll be fine!

# **Stubbornness**

For some, trading is a battle. Trading is a war! Because trading is about being right. One man taking on the world. A one-man army, doing battle with the forces of economic stupidity, corporate mendacity, financial… something-y.

I think, because it is difficult to take on the world in your underpants, I have somehow managed to avoid this.

But even I can be stubborn at times.

"I can make money where others can't. I know it all."

It's what lots of us think from time to time. A feeling of stubbornness or superiority is a real problem when it comes to making money in the markets.

Here's a real-life example:

Andy's tale

Despite being told endlessly by me that nearly all traders who bet on the FTSE 100 and other indices going up or down lose over time (shorting for brief bear market periods is something else), Andy was determined that he was the one that could do it.

He bragged to others at one of the breaks at a seminar I was running:

"I've made nearly £2,000 so far today. It's like taking candy from a baby..."

There are two problems here. Firstly, he was trying to persuade other people to gamble like him and ignore my stuff! Secondly, that baby he was stealing from was actually the kid from the movie *Omen* and Andy was playing with his trading life.

Later on in the day I could see he was starting to look cross. I asked him how it was going.

"I made a lot on the FTSE," he said, "but now I am losing on the Dow. It spiked down while I was having a coffee and fag outside."

I made no comment. He carried on. He ended the day having lost a lot. I made a comment as to whether day trading the indices was really a good idea.

"Doing what I do," he said, "you have to take big losses sometimes. It's the name of the game."

The actual name of the game here is *Being Too Stubborn to Trade Well*. It's also sometimes known as *Being a Bit of a Plonker*. It's like *Cluedo* but the one who ends up dead is you.

Three months later he sent me a sorry tale of massive losses and how he had blown up all his accounts with betting on the FTSE. You'd have thought he would be a little bit shamefaced. He wasn't:

"I know where I went wrong," he wrote. "And when I've got some money again, I know exactly how I will trade the FTSE."

With some people, you just have to give up or they'll drive you out of your Vulcan mind!

Getting stuck

I can't tell you the number of times I have heard non-sharks say things like "I am stuck with this one", "I feel trapped", "I can't possibly sell it now."

The moment I say something like, "What do you mean, stuck with it?" they look shocked. The idea that they might not be stuck with it doesn't even occur to them. They haven't contemplated selling.

The non-shark way is easy to buy, hard to sell. The shark way is buy if it really looks good, sell if it starts to lose.

Can you imagine Mr Spock's raised eyebrow if Kirk told him he'd bought an oil stock and had held onto it and it was now showing a 70% loss? I suspect he would say, "Captain, that is simply not logical."

Even Kirk would struggle to get out of that fix. Well, he could by selling.

Psychologically having a portfolio that looks like this is demoralising and certainly would show no shark or Spock-like attributes:

-17%
+7%
-70%
+23%
-82%
-12%
+3%
-37%
-44%

This portfolio was shown to me by a real trader. He couldn't figure out where he was going wrong – he had bought some "great stocks" with "amazing potential".

On suggesting they were losers and he should sell them he looked at me as if I was totally bonkers.

"No, goodness, those are going to come back – there's no point taking a loss on them now."

Why weren't there more winners?

"Well, I tend to bank winners quite quickly to cover some of the bigger losses."

That doesn't make sense.

"Once a winner gets to 10% I am out of there."

Er, good luck!

He just didn't seem to think he was doing much wrong. If the oil price jumped, his smaller oil shares could easily double in a day or two, thus making his portfolio a big winner. But that was delusional. In effect he was cutting his profits and running his losses, the opposite of what he should be doing.

After building more than £1 million in an ISA with a major broker, I recently started another ISA with a new execution-only broker. It was cheaper on costs and I liked the platform. I thought it would be interesting to try it out for a while. So far I have managed to make the 25% or so that I am after every year.

Here's how that looks:

+18%
+7%
+5%
+40%
-8%
+72%
+81%
+4%
+12%
+21%
+3%
-6%

I am running profits. Anything that grew into a loss of more than 10% in the account has been ruthlessly chopped. I have bought a wide spread of different companies. The ones down 6% and 8% have got a little longer to prove themselves but will be cut if they go down much more than 10%.

If any of the big profits get to 100%, I'll topslice some unemotionally. This also ensures one share doesn't have a massively bigger weighting than any of the others (increasing risk unnecessarily).

I haven't bought any bonkers oil or commodity stocks. It would now be pretty hard to lose all that 25%. Stop-losses on the winners can be placed at least at break-even, some can now be placed at places that mean I should win big even if the share comes down.

I don't have to watch the screen on this portfolio all day.

Overtrading

A common subset of stubbornness is **overtrading**. It can also come about because of boredom or negative feelings – there is such a thing as 'comfort trading'. A trade is a chance for something good to happen, after all.

I'm dealing with it in this chapter because I think comfort trades are really related to stubbornness. We may put them on when we're feeling low, but the positive effect we're seeking is ultimately one that satisfies our stubbornness.

A reader called Sheila sums up the problem of overtrading and the solution really well:

"In January, I doubt I am the only girl trader who has made the connection between success in dieting and success in trading. A bit of willpower goes a long way in both cases. If I decide to lose a few dietary pounds I adopt a mindset where I am disciplined, focused and let nothing, not even one small biscuit, slip through the net. My desire to lose weight is stronger than all my conflicting emotional urges to tuck into rubbish and slowly but surely the scales start to move the right way. The same is true of trading. If I transfer my weight-loss mindset to my trading activity, slowly but surely those accounts start to build.

"Unfortunately, the reverse is also true. Comfort trading is a close relative of comfort eating, only more expensive. You can picture the scene – I'm sure we've all been there. Maybe despite my best efforts a run of trades just didn't work out, maybe I've had a bad morning and a black cloud is sitting over my head. Whatever the reason, I let my guard down and before I know it my emotions have the upper hand and I decide to trade my way out of it, grabbing a quick chocolate bar as I go. Guess what, I'm comfort trading. What I'm looking for is a few quick fixes to prove to myself and all those other doubters that I can be a successful trader and that I know how to take the rough with the smooth.

"But it doesn't work out that way and I end up feeling even worse. Even with tight stops, it's amazing how these snatched trades (usually spread bets) and their losses can rack up. Really, who needs it?

"No one extra trade and no one extra chocolate bar on its own is going to be catastrophic (probably) but if I want to shift those extra pounds I really do have to turn down those carbs each and every day and if I want to make money I really do have to stop making comfort trades."

Anger

The Incredible Hulk might have turned green when he got angry, but when traders lose it their accounts invariably turn red – and stay that way.

Anger is one of the hardest emotions in the world to get over. For traders, it generally strikes when we have been attempting to make money on a share – and every time we have tried to make money out of it, it has ended up a loser.

I have known some shares drive traders absolutely potty.

This is the usual scenario: A trader buys a share. He is convinced said share is fantastic. Said share proves to be less than fantastic and promptly falls. The trader cuts his losses. The share falls further. The trader gets tempted... I mean, it really does look fantastic... and buys back in. The share keeps falling. The trader gets a grip and sells. The share goes back up. Frustrated, he buys. It falls. Infuriated, he buys. It still falls. He still buys! It falls and falls... There is only so much averaging down a man can do; he sells. It goes up.

Goodness, he buys!

Each time the trade ends with a loss. The more the share loses him, the more he is determined to win back.

Sharks would quickly realise what is happening: they want to take revenge on the share.

Three strikes and you're out

I've met a lot of people that this has happened to. It's very common. It is a saintly person who doesn't want a bit of revenge when they feel they have been wronged. But most of us manage to restrain the feeling in real life, or the murder rate would be higher.

In trading, though, not only do you have to hold back from feelings of revenge, you can't even afford to secretly nurture them. The consequences of trying to slaughter a share into submission are so much less than slaughtering your neighbour with the overgrown Wisteria, that the temptation is too dangerous. We should not have those feelings at all.

So many have struggled with this, and I have felt the pull myself, that I have a ruthless answer. It is totally non-negotiable: three strikes and you are out! If you trade a share three times and get it wrong, leave that share alone.

For at least six months, don't even check its price. And if it made you really mad, maybe forget it forever. This is the only way to cope. Three and out.

You tried three times to make money out of a share and failed. Now take the share off your screen and do *not* be tempted to even take a look at it.

If you don't, I can almost guarantee you'll be back in it and obsessed. You'll spend way too much time on the one share, watching its every move, hoping this time you'll make something out of it.

Even worse, you may end up averaging down in it. This can lead to some serious lost cash. I have been there myself! As related in my book *The Naked Trader,* I bought shares in Coffee Republic. (Never did any research beyond, er, liking the coffee. Do'h!)

I bought at all prices down from 28p, eventually selling at 3p, losing myself more than £8,000. If I traded like a shark then (I definitely didn't) I'd have tried three times then been out.

Regret

Vulcans are thoughtful by nature. By and large this is positive. It's good to consider the possibilities of a trade going the other way; of what you'll do when a share goes down or up; of making sure you carve out time in the day to eat enough Twixes to keep you fuelled.

There is one deadly side effect of being thoughtful, though. It is when you get an attack of the 'What ifs'.

The 'What ifs' are a terrible affliction. They can lead you into awful trades. At heart, they are emotional, even if they feel like intellectual angst. Their basis is in regret.

But Mr Spock has no regrets. No shark ever does.

'Why oh why did I do this or not do that? What if I had done this instead? What if I had done that? What if, what if, what if…'

Giving into regrets is a gateway to many of the other emotions we've discussed. It makes a trader angry, fearful, stubborn, egomaniacal – and pretty soon, a gambler, a total trading lunatic.

> "Fear of Regret – An inability to accept that you've made a wrong decision, which leads to holding onto losers too long or selling winners too soon."
>
> **Gavin McQuill**

I have a lot of 'What ifs' come into my head all the time. I can't stop them. 'What if I had bought this share last year?', 'What if I had run profits on that share rather than selling it?', 'What if I had bought marmalade instead of strawberry jam?'

But I dismiss them right away.

The 'What ifs' draw you back to shares you shouldn't be interested in any more.

A stiff G&T

An example: Fever-Tree (producer of posh tonics and mixers) came onto the market in the same week as Quartix (vehicle trackers) in November 2014. Two new issues at the time and I was interested in both! But I only had spare cash in my ISA to buy one of them. I pondered and bought Quartix. Hindsight tells me I should have bought both.

The Quartix trade went well and I doubled my money on it. But Fever-Tree! If I had bought that I would have *quadrupled* my money. I could think on and on about it and beat myself up. But that's the wrong thing to do. It makes no sense.

Now that I have spare cash, I might try and buy Fever-Tree because I regret not buying it earlier – but any share is a different proposition when it's a different price. (And even when it's the same price but at a different time.) This could be the wrong time or the wrong price or both. It could be on a big high. I mustn't just go back and buy it because the initial investment case was strong a while ago.

I summoned up the Vulcan blood and managed to banish the 'What ifs'. The best way to do this, I find, is to pretend I have never seen the share before: can I build an investment case from scratch? What would it take for the share to be a good buy again? Don't have regrets: plan for the future instead.

The 'What ifs' can also make you trade rashly in other shares in order to get over the regret of mistakes or missing out. The good thing is, once you're aware of the role regret can play, you'll soon notice when it's whispering in your ear to trade, trade, trade.

A reader of mine had a similar experience with Fever-Tree. He has come to a very healthy perspective on regret:

John's tale

"When I see a company make a big jump I think 'If only I had bought the day before' and work out what it would be worth now. Take Fever-Tree. When it was an IPO I did not buy it. I like Fever-Tree's products and should have gone with my own instinct and what you say in your book: invest in what you know and like [You also have to make sure it's a good company! – Robbie]. Since then it has done very well.

"I worked out that if I had sold my £30,000 portfolio and put all my money into Fever-Tree it would have returned me £120,000.

"But this is torture and completely futile! I would *never* sell all my shares and put all my money into just one company!

"What helped me understand this clearly was the realisation that basing my figures on hindsight is just the same as saying 'If only I had picked those lottery numbers yesterday.'

"And when I notice a share that nosedives I don't think 'I'm glad I never had those.'"

John is so right. Torturing yourself over trades you woulda, coulda, shoulda made is futile. If you're going to do that, you might as well congratulate yourself on the millions of bad decisions you didn't make. Just concentrate on the next opportunity to come along.

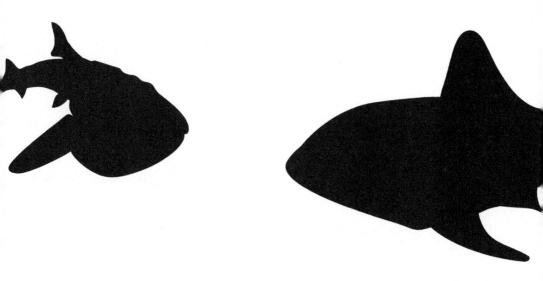

PART III:
Danger Zones and Traps

Classic Dangers

If you trade like a shark, you obviously hope you will be a pretty dangerous character. But you won't be the only shark – or predator – out there. There are lots of dangerous creatures in the financial markets and some of them are quite a bit bigger than sharks.

Don't think that Spock had it any easier. Space might be the final frontier; but it's also the place where no one can hear you scream. The markets are similar. There's no limit to the possibilities – there are fortunes to be made! But you can also end up getting your throat torn out by the retractable jaws of slime-covered, acid-blooded strangers (I think the technical term is hedge fund managers).

And no one will hear you – or help you.

That's why I've written the next few chapters. In part II we looked at how emotions inside us can lead us astray. In this part we're going to look out how outside influences can play havoc with our trading minds. There are lots of dangers out there just waiting to exploit your brain – some old, some new – but there are also simple ways you can protect yourself.

Investing misconceptions

Conventional wisdom can kill. Peter Lynch is a hugely respected American investor and writer. He came up with 12 of the worst things most investors believe. These are things that lots of us like to trot out. They seem like common sense but they only lead to common mistakes. Sharks know this and refuse to pay attention to them.

Here they are:

1. 'If it's gone down this much already it can't go much lower'

I don't even know how many times I have heard this, especially from those who have fallen in love with stocks or are bottom pickers.

Other phrases I hear about stocks that have gone down a lot are: "I may as well stay with it", or "I am trapped in it". Sharks would never be in this position in the first place – they get out early because there is no law that says a share can't keep falling.

2. 'You can always tell when a stock's hit bottom'

History has proven this wrong countless times. If it was that easy, people wouldn't have just sold out to bring the price that low, would they?

Lynch talks about this being like trying to catch a falling knife. It ends up with you heading to the trading equivalent of A&E.

3. 'If it's gone this high already, how can it possibly go higher?'

If you sell a company whenever it doubles you won't get to enjoy a 'ten bagger'. A shark way of looking at this is simply to **topslice**: sell 20% perhaps, bank a few gains, but leave the rest to roll on.

You should also always use a trailing stop.

If a company's share price keeps rising it could simply be because profits are rising! And that might keep going for years. An example from my own trading is GB Group. It's gone from 25p to 250p over seven years. There were hundreds of times along the way that anyone might have said: 'It's only common sense that it can't go higher.' They would have been wrong, and poorer if they acted on it.

GB Group – can it go any higher?

4. 'It's only $3 a share: what can I lose?'

A cheap share is not the same as a good share. No one thinks anything cheap is automatically good when out shopping, or Poundland would be John Lewis' biggest rival.

5. 'Eventually they always come back'

I can't even tell you how many times I have heard someone say a share "will come back", as if they are certain it will. They can't believe it dropped in the first place and are sure it will rise again but as Lynch points out it could go bust. Many do.

6. 'It's always darkest before the dawn'

Lynch looks at freight-car deliveries (in the UK I guess we would call these goods wagons... it's been a long time since I watched *Thomas the Tank Engine*) – an industry that fell 90% over the years 1979 to 1983.

Throughout those four years, Lynch wonders how many investors kept telling themselves things couldn't go any lower. It was the same with the 2007–8 banking crash... things really did just keep getting worse. A recent example would be the oil price falling from $125 to $28 as I write this in early 2016.

I guess the point here is that it is very hard to catch a turnaround – sharks would wait first.

7. 'When it rebounds to $10, I'll sell'

This is very common amongst the Kirks of this world. The desperate hope of a bounce should not keep you in. You trade because you believe in a share. This is knowing a trade is dead but sticking with it anyway.

8. 'Conservative stocks don't fluctuate much'

Many safe FTSE 100 shares have halved quite readily – a good example is Tesco, many considered it a conservative stock ("everyone needs food") but it still halved in value.

9. 'It's taking too long for anything to ever happen'

I understand why traders get tired of a share doing nothing very much. It ties up money which you could be using to make profits elsewhere. But then, you bought those shares for a reason and they may eventually start moving. And perhaps they have dividends in the meantime...

So sitting tight can be the best thing. (Not always – it may depend on other opportunities.) A shark will definitely have a stop-loss on boring shares, though, in case when they finally start moving they do so by... falling.

10. 'Look at all the money I've lost by not buying that'

Everyone thinks this. Well, except sharks. Indeed sharks tend to take these stocks off their screens in case they are tempted into a non-shark buy when it is too high.

11. 'I missed that one but I'll catch the next one'

Investors miss the next big thing and wait around for the next one rather than seeing if the opportunity they missed still makes sense for them to invest in. Sometimes it can.

12. 'The stock's gone up so I must be right, or... the stock's gone down so I must be wrong'

There isn't really such a thing as right or wrong in the markets. It is all a matter of simply going with it but knowing when to cut if it goes wrong.

It is interesting that huge wealth can be created by simply holding onto the winners, sometimes for many years. Steve Jobs became rich by holding onto one stock. His salary was $1. Luck was involved – and a good business brain to make his company worth so much – but a shark always remembers that bigger money can come from holding a small amount of very good stocks.

I met a guy worth a fortune at an event and I asked him for the secret of his success. He said:

> "Oh, I just bought Mobil shares 40 years ago and held on. I still have the certificates. Once in a while I sell a few if I need to..."

There was an element of luck in buying those shares when he did – but he still had the logic to carry on holding them. And I suspect most ISA millionaires have just done the same thing: managed to hold on to a good proportion of good shares for a long time.

That's what I did. I mentioned GB Group earlier in this chapter – that share has garnered me more than £100,000 in profits. It's gone up more than ten times. I topsliced some along the way, like a good shark, but also added as it went up slowly over the years.

Another one was Dialight – all the way from 150p in 2008 through to 1400p by 2013. I didn't actually get out at the top but I ended up with a stop-loss sitting 150p under the price, which got me out of most at 1250 and 1150ish, to bank in excess of £150,000.

Dialight – banking £150,000 profit

Theory vs practice

In his excellent book on trading psychology, *Your Money And Your Brain*, Jason Zweig argues: "You will never maximise your wealth unless you can optimise your mind."

I think this is true. As we've covered, your mind has to be super sharp and free of all clutter to make it.

Zweig also suggests it is all very well to have 'theory' but humans usually end up doing the exact opposite in practice.

For example, in theory: "You have clear and consistent financial goals."

In practice: "You're not sure what your goals are. The last time you thought you knew, you had to change them."

Three of Zweig's false investing theories are ones that I have come across a lot among traders. The thing is – in theory – these theories make sense. (If you see what I mean.) But in practice, it all falls apart.

They are actually theories that people progressing towards full Vulcan citizenship are more prone to believing precisely because they all sound so logical.

Here they are:

Theory: "You carefully calculate the odds of success and failure."

Practice: "That stock your cousin recommended was a 'sure thing' till it shocked you both by going to zero."

As a Vulcan or shark in training, you have honed your rational skills. You meticulously work out how much you are prepared to lose and what you want to win and how and when.

Well, until you see the stock going down and decide to give it a 'little more legroom'. Then some more. Now we get the 'stick with it, it will come back' routine… then your plan is gone and you realise being a shark is going to take a lot more work.

Theory: "The smarter you are, the more money you will make."

Practice: "In 1720, Sir Isaac Newton was wiped out in a stock market crash, blazing a trail of financial failure that geniuses have been following ever since."

Yes, indeed. You can be smart all right but it doesn't mean a thing in the markets. Someone in a low job with little education can make a lot more than someone with all the qualifications in the world. I have seen it! We are all equals in trading.

Theory: "The more closely you follow your investments, the more money you will make."

Practice: "People who keep up with the news about their stocks earn lower returns than those who pay almost no attention."

This might seem a strange one. But sharks know that if you follow every little move on your stock of choice, the chances are you will take too much action at the wrong time. Stay interested, sure, but you should also stay out of its face. Stick to your pre-determined stops rather than fretting.

Other people and their advice

Sam's tale

Here is a story from Sam. He has a terrible tale of losing nearly a million:

"In September/October 2007 I was very nervous about the financial markets and I sold virtually all my shares. I had well over seven figures in cash.

"In March 2008, a relative came to visit his mum and stayed with us. After dinner he told me he had four of the best shares he had ever seen and that I should mortgage all I had and put it into them. He ran through the reasons why. The following morning (I believe that after dinner is not the best time to get advice on shares) he showed me, again, why he had invested heavily in each of them.

"He also said that, because he had such substantial holdings, he would be able to keep track of them and keep me up to date.

When I said that I was in cash because I didn't trust the markets at that time, he said that precisely these shares would flourish even in that market.

"The shares never reached the same level again. When they started to go down I kept asking him for advice on what to do (instead of doing what every bone in my body was telling me to do: follow Robbie's advice, get out now). Each time he said hang on, they're fine, they're going to come right (in more detail, of course, with attractive price targets for the end of the year etc.). Within three months I had lost virtually all my capital. The shares were down 90%.

"I had kept a couple of hundred thousand back, of course; I'm not totally stupid (or maybe I am) but when the upturn came I still had those four losers and he was still telling me that they were going to come right. They never have, of course. I was like a rabbit in the headlights. I didn't dare do anything, believing that he was far wiser than I was and not daring to use the cash I had held back in the market, as I still had to clothe, feed, house and educate my family.

"So I've watched the markets rise over the past seven years, unable to do anything about it. I didn't dare risk the cash I had held back in the market. I needed it to live. It has, of course, disappeared at an alarming rate on living, while the markets have left me far behind.

"You don't need me to draw the lessons from this:

- "Greed, of course. Cash was unproductive while here was a successful professional telling me how to (at least) double my money within a year.

- "Failing to get out when the shares had fallen 5% or 10% (the maximum I would normally accept).

- "Listening to advice and believing anything other than one's own independent research (he was a chartered accountant with a

Big Five firm before going into banking/investment, and share analysis was his speciality).

- "Continuing to listen as the shares sank, and sank, and sank (the damage was done in three months – during which I didn't sleep very much and continued to believe what I was being told. Wanting to believe it and telling myself that he had millions at stake…).

- "With hindsight, not investing the cash I had when the market turned. I would have made back my losses sticking to the principles you teach.

"And the psychology of all this? You're better placed than I am to work that out. But the money I lost is money that I earned; most of it by working and the rest by careful investing. Following the very simple rules you preach and researching, for myself, many of the firms you yourself have found."

This is an amazingly honest story from Sam. It is very kind of him to share it with everyone and it is a big lesson on how things can go badly wrong if you pay too much attention to **other people's advice**.

Emotionally, it's very easy to do because it feels so logical… and activates lots of other emotions like greed – but that's just a *feeling*, not a reason!

Someone he respected had told him he was going to double his money – so why not give it a go? It is very hard for humans not to be influenced by others. I have had meals with people trying to persuade me into all sorts of non-shark behaviour (usually egging me on to buy a dodgy oil share) – I smile politely and don't do anything.

Sam could still have turned this around. He could have told his friend: "OK I will try it but I am having a 15% stop on it as I don't want to lose more on these companies if something bad happens."

Doing that even after the initial mistake would have saved Sam most of his money. But I think he was 'in it together' with his friend. Soon, most of the money was gone.

Sam had blown it after some good years of carefully researched investment. He had been doing the right thing. And that goes to show how hard it can be to retain shark status. One must be wary at all times of getting into bad habits. It doesn't matter if you stray occasionally. But you need to be mindful if you start to stray a lot. If Sam had treated his million in a business-like way he could not have lost most of it.

When I got my ISA to a million I was determined to hang on to most of it – if it had gone down to £750,000 I would have sold everything and taken a break as something must have been going wrong. Sam couldn't face the markets anymore with the last of his money, and though he wishes he had gone back in, he is quite right about not going back. He needed that money and you should never trade with money you cannot afford to lose.

I would like to thank Sam for this tale. Hopefully you can learn the lessons he learned the hard way. Sam sent me a final email summing up what he thinks were his emotional problems:

"The error was, of course, mine – taking his advice and making those investments. For that I have no one to blame but myself. What I find difficult to forgive him for, on the other hand, is continuing, during and after the precipitous drop, to tell me that he had firsthand information on all the shares because of his big holdings and that I should just hang on; that everything would come right.

"The lesson, of course, is yours – never ever betray the principles you teach. Be ruthless in getting out of shares which do not perform as you have planned for them. Take the loss. Two things stopped me doing that: the speed and the size of the loss (which should not have been a factor) and the fact that I believed that someone who was paid $20m a year knew better than I did.

"There will be times when one can stretch the rules, of course. But those times are few and concern certain very specific cases. When analysis gives good reasons to hang onto a share which has dropped further than one expected. But even there, the safe thing is to get out. As you say, there's always another good share on its way. Preserve capital.

"A corollary of this has been that, three years ago, I gave some cash I had in the USA to professional managers to handle, no longer trusting myself. Initially they did very well indeed. But I've just returned from New York where I learnt that that too has been a disaster.

"I have never made money other than by selling the few talents I have – working; and by prudent investing. Of this last, following your advice to the letter has been the most productive. Deviation from it, a disaster. One has to respect the capital (preserve it) and be ruthless in dealing with anything which threatens it."

Being led by others is a terrible mistake. However convincing these people are, you have to be careful of other people and their 'advice'.

Fred's tale

In a similar but not so dramatic vein, reader Fred got influenced too:

> "A friend of mine had been 'tipped off' (!) that some shares were about to rocket imminently. You can guess what happened... as the shares nose-dived my friend invested more cash as he was informed that they were about to turn, and then more cash, and then persuaded me to do the same. And then, well, you get the picture. We kept on putting in cash till we both lost the lot when they reached rock bottom.

> "We don't talk about it anymore, through embarrassment I'd guess, from the conversations we had at the time I think he lost over £15,000 and I lost £10,000."

Do not mix friendships with trading. Keep friends for having fun. Trading is a business, not a social thing. It's not something you do for a bit of a laugh.

Part of this means you shouldn't boast when you win or moan when you lose either, as we discussed earlier. Your friends will inevitably want to know more... and they could start to influence you even without meaning to.

Baa baa bad trader, have you any stock picks

Humans are pack animals. We want to be part of a group. Be recognised by our peers. Do the same as others. We don't want to be left out... baa!

Did you ever see Mr Spock just follow what everyone else was doing? I don't think so. Remember how many silly mistakes Kirk made, and how often Spock would logically go against him? Granted, sometimes Kirk won through against all logic – but in trading it won't work. If you're currently being a sheep, you have to stop your baa-ad behaviour.

Sheep are likely to try and follow:

Tipsters

No, tipsters aren't those men with big beards who live in Shoreditch.

Think spiv. Tipsters just want your lovely direct debit payments coming into their bank accounts every month or year. Even better, once you are out of the market and nursing your losses, you'll forget to cancel the direct debit.

A tipster from a certain well-known publication told me that they more or less live off forgotten direct debits. It doesn't really matter what the tipsters pick. And their stats are easily massaged to suit.

Journalists

There are acres of writing in the business pages by journalists – tipping shares, discussing companies, evaluating sectors. And plenty of magazines too. All urging you that this or that looks a great buy, or this or that is one to avoid. It all looks great, the journos look like they have done their homework.

Now, don't get me wrong: I think some magazines, like *Investors Chronicle* and *Shares*, are great to read for ideas and news. But when it comes to some of the other publications out there and all those exciting tips you see around the place… you have to stop and think. Why has a journo been slaving away on a mag for years and years on £35,000 a year when if they were really good they'd be sitting at home earning £100,000 or more from their own amazing tips?

There are good magazines out there, and good journalists, but there are also lots of bad ones.

Brokers

You'll see a lot of broker reports getting mentions in the news and online. Upgrades, downgrades, buys and holds. But you won't get to see these till their clients have and share prices have already gone up or down.

Again, simply ignore this noise. If brokers really knew what they were talking about do you think they would (a) continue commuting into an office every day, or (b) take their laptop to Barbados and stay there? (PS. It's 'b'.)

Bulletin board gurus

Sheep really favour bulletin boards. Bulletin board gurus get a following, often by being charismatic writers. But in reality they just want you to buy what they're buying because it all helps to push up a share in which they have invested.

Many also try 'pumping and dumping', which is finding a tiny penny share, buying it, then pushing it (pumping) before selling it (dumping) while continuing to push it. Then never mentioning it again when it retreats back down.

I have heard from countless people who have been sucked into holding other people's dumps. Yes, it is as upsetting as it sounds.

Copy-me sites

This is a new thing: copy-me sites. Sites that enable you to copy the best trader and all that. It's funny but I have never heard of anyone copying anyone else for a long time and always making money.

Me!

Yes, that's right! You may be tempted to follow me. After all, I make regular money from the markets – why not just lob money on some of the stuff I buy? The thing is, I could win with some of those shares and you might still lose.

Huh? How's that?

By the time I put a buy up on my site it might already be up quite a bit. I certainly hope so or I wouldn't have bloody bought it!

By the time you come to sell, I might already have been out for a good profit. Or I might have already taken a quick loss on it. And if I picked a stinker – and I certainly have picked some – I will have exited, shark-like, for a small loss. But you might still be hanging on because I haven't updated my site yet. (I do have a day-job, after all. Sitting around in my underwear takes dedication.)

The thing is, I am not trying to provide a share-tipping service or even be remotely up-to-the-minute. I am just keeping a long-term public record of what I have done over time in order to show you that anyone – if they follow simple rules and discipline – can make money the same way I have (by following simple rules and discipline!).

I don't want you to copy me! I didn't make money by copying others. I don't make money by you copying me. No one benefits. (And if I did, it would be dodgy as hell and still not something to recommend.) It makes no sense. Please don't try it!

People in pubs

Funnily enough, you shouldn't pay attention to the financial advice of anyone consuming alcohol.

You should also avoid the hot share tips of anyone standing around by the office water cooler.

It amazes me how many times I hear someone has bought something because a mate's mate's best friend told someone at his work to buy such and such. It is very appealing. You feel like you're being passed a secret.

"Keep this quiet, but I've heard a company is going to be bid for, it's probably going to go up 50% – you *will* keep it quiet though, right?"

Here's a tale from Richard:

"It was my first ever trade. A bloke at work said his wife heard about this share from someone and it was going to rocket. I bought blind and it went down. It then went down a load more and I still have it down 80%. The bloke at work has been keeping a very low profile since I bought it."

(Sell, Richard, sell!)

I remember one bloke who came to a seminar who told me "someone down the pub" had told him to buy an oil share called Xcite Energy when it was about three quid. He regaled me with stories of how the pub bloke knew oil was about to gush out of ... well, wherever they were drilling and yes, OK, he had lost 30% so far but had now been told to, "Buy more... it's not long before the good news comes out."

You can guess what happened. Xcite Energy, far from being 'xciting' plummeted in the months after.

Children with Ferraris

A little while ago I kept getting emails about a story in the papers regarding a teenager boasting of having turned £2,000 into £21m. His local paper had run a story where he claimed to be a self-made multimillionaire from trading in the stock market. He was pictured with a Ferrari.

I remember the people writing to me who wanted exactly the same thing. If a spotty teenager could turn £2,000 into £21 million THEY COULD TOO!

I explained that it was obviously a scam – it was an impossible feat for anyone, even using leverage. Think about it. His claim was:

- March 2014: Using a £2,000 loan from his father he traded in German debt to make £23,000.

- May 2014: More trades in America and Italy make him £100,000.

- July 2014: A series of lucrative trades take his value to £6m.

- January 2015: More deals take his wealth to £17.5m by the autumn and £21m by the start of 2015.

Total crap! When I explained this to my correspondents I could feel their disappointment. I also felt they were still inclined to believe the too-good-to-be-true story. I was pricking their dream bubble. They were excited and there I was, a boring old fart telling them the best they could probably get out of £2,000 was £500.

Well, after three months the admiring emails regarding the wunderkind trader died off. I remembered it a few months later when I came across this headline: "Teenage fraudster jailed for stock market con".

Even worse, he had taken money off people who believed he was going to invest it for them. He conned them out of £110,000.

How was he caught? An alert copper spotted his Ferrari was a fake! He was jailed for two years.

If it's too good to be true, don't be a prat

The fact this little git could get so much money off would-be investors shows how easily a lot of people are conned and why, again, any shark treats anything too good to be true in the stock market as cobblers.

It really is hard not to believe in something you really want to believe in, especially if you think it will improve your life. I spent the weekend once with a total conman who, despite the fact he openly admitted he was one and had spent time in jail, quite easily obtained money from investors. I decided to meet him because I was fascinated to understand his total lack of morality. I found it interesting that he quite simply didn't care who he conned, he thought they were idiots to be robbed. And like all conmen, he was totally charming. It was worth spending the time with him to understand how the mind of someone like that worked.

Someone else who met him that day wrote to me bemoaning the fact that he had lost money. Frankly, I wasn't sympathetic. If you give money to a conman who openly says he is a conman and you're surprised when he runs off with the money... Well, honestly!

The guy who conned people really didn't care. He thought if people were stupid enough to fall for it, more fool them. Their money provided him with lots of funds to gamble with on the poker tables.

According to the papers, he got his comeuppance when he 'invested' £200,000 for someone who it turns out was holding the money for a gangster. Cue the conman promptly disappearing and someone with a gun turning up at his hideout...

Prophets

Sharks are aware that the future cannot be reliably predicted, not even with the help of the past. Things happen that no one could expect.

One 'forecaster' took me out to lunch once. "I always tell one newspaper the FTSE is going to go up this year and another it is going to go down," he said.

"At the year end, the one I was right with says how brilliant I was, the one I got it wrong with just doesn't mention it, so it is a win–win situation."

You should take all those who pretend to know what will happen with a massive pinch of salt or do what sharks do – ignore them.

A recent example of something no one really forecast is the dramatic fall in the oil price, still ongoing in early 2016 as I write this. You heard it everywhere: the wailing and gnashing of teeth as it kept on going down despite the forecasters forecasting it wouldn't carry on going down.

Non-sharks stayed with their oil stocks; the more they went down the more they stayed with them. I have plenty of those sorts of stories.

This was from Phil:

> "Unfortunately one of my worst trades is still ongoing – Xcite Energy [That share again! – Robbie]. I bought in at less than £1 and rode it up to £3+, sold some, watched it fall back, but because I still liked the idea of their proven oil reserves I decided to buy a load more at around £1, not expecting the oil price to collapse. Hey ho."

Hey ho? Never hey ho! Hey ho is the equivalent of a shrug of the shoulders. Never shrug the shoulders. It means you aren't taking action when you can and should be. And there's the word "expecting". You should never 'expect' anything – sharks look at cold hard figures. And respond logically and immediately.

No one knows the future

It is a fact of life – and an important reason that you can actually make money in the markets – that no one knows the future.

Well, except that kid on *Back to the Future*.

It's a shame. I wish I could go back to 2007 and short all the banks... But not even the people who run the economy know what is going to happen next. Sharks understand that. The Bank of England kept saying interest rates were going to go up time and time again and at the time of writing they still haven't. No one bar a few clever guys (see or read *The Big Short*) saw the US housing crash coming.

And in any event the stock market is bonkers and can over-value or under-value things for a long time, more time than you have money to cover it if you're wrong.

Predictions about anything in the market should be ignored. Sharks realise this – they are not interested in having a guess, they will simply follow events rather than thinking they know everything.

It must (not) be love

You simply must not ever fall in love with a share.

You may like a company's product or shops or the sector it's in, but if the shares start to go down you have to get out.

A good example of this would be Hornby. Older men especially had a nostalgic feeling for the company that made the train sets they had played with when younger (and older).

These men would buy Hornby shares out of sheer love. Forgetting trading is an unemotional business, they stayed with the shares, even though kids were more interested in iPads and computer games than toy trains. Profit warning after profit warning flashed by like broken signals – the share heading for the end of the line with no brakes...

Some people fall in love with one or two shares and watch them all day long. But shares are *not* a relationship and they should be dumped if they are not performing.

The little things

So conventional wisdom, other people's advice and falling in love are the big classic threats. But there are littler classic threats too. In closing this chapter, these are the most common and the easiest to fix in my experience:

Clear your mind? Clear your desk!

Believe me, I am a right messy sod. There are times when my desk has toast plates, old tea cups, jam smears and all kinds of nasty bits and pieces floating about – and that's when I find I just can't concentrate and I cease to be Mr Spock. There is something about chocolate stains that brings out the Kirk in me.

Once I've cleaned it up I feel a lot better.

Had a drink? Don't trade

Been out for lunch and had a few crafty beers? Flush with confidence, now is an excellent time to trade if you want to lose money.

Emotional bust-up? Step away from the laptop

Life can be cruel at times. If you've been dumped, or done the dumping, had someone close to you die – anything like that, leave trading alone till you have healed a bit.

Feeling pissed off about anything? Try not to trade!

The results aren't pretty.

Digital Dangers

Once upon a time most people reading this would only be able to trade by ringing up their stockbroker (er, I mean, flipping open their communicators to send subspace transmissions).

The digital revolution has been great – trading has never been simpler, cheaper, quicker.

Or more deadly, if you aren't aware of the digital dangers out there. These are the tech-related difficulties that threaten your mind when trading.

Let me help you lose everything

Newbies to the stock market soon find themselves surrounded by people or firms looking to help them lose all their money. Even experienced traders aren't always safe. These dodgy companies and characters play on our emotions, you see.

You'll see ads everywhere from Forex brokers, providers, trainers, systems... "Make £1,000 a day," they cry. (You might lose £1,000 a day.) "Become a millionaire!" (You might lose your home.)

For some reason it's almost always Forex or currency trading they try to get you with. Their method of attack is invariably digital: through ads, emails, paid-for articles, videos.

You won't find anyone else writing this. That's because I'm a free agent – I don't need to take money from the Forex industry. I can tell it as it is. Most websites get a lot of cash from their ads and can't accept articles slagging off the very people sending them dough.

I just tell them that I know nearly everyone loses trading Forex, which is why I tell people to avoid it, which is why I would be a pretty disgusting hypocrite to promote it, wouldn't I?

I can't even count how many stories I have been told by people who have lost playing Forex and similar markets. Guess what lots of them say when I tell them they'll always lose at Forex?

"Only 99% lose. I can be the 1% that makes it."

You're gonna need a bigger boat if you believe that. A dreadnought, perhaps. Or an aircraft carrier.

Sharks know that flashy, whizzy, sexy things like trading your way to millions through Forex are a load of nonsense. Faced with the digital danger of all the enticing ads and systems and sponsored content out there, they resolve never to trade:

- binary markets
- Forex
- gold
- metals
- Bitcoins
- oil

- indices (unless a short hedge – explained in chapter 4)

- sports events

- penny shares

- small oil shares

- commodities in general.

Sharks, instead, are happy to embrace:

- sectors

- medium-sized companies

- smaller companies with prospects

- companies paying good dividends

- FTSE shorts in bad times

- investment trusts

- decent funds.

New tech madness

There's something about new technology that hijacks traders' minds. While some of it is a big help (I officially recommend a new invention, it's called the internet), if you go over the top it becomes a lot less useful. Traders seem to think the latest, most-up-to-date technical things will inevitably make them better traders. They'll be faster, more informed, more flexible.

Don't make that mistake.

In the 1950s, Nicolas Darvas was a touring dancer in the United States. After studying some classic investment books, Darvas started trading shares… and shortly managed to trade his way to $2m (about $16m in today's terms).[2]

---

2   You can read his story in his book at **www.harriman-house.com/how-i-made-2-million-in-the-stock-market-2**

Here's the thing: because he was touring, Darvas had to rely on week-old editions of the financial pages to make his trades. And he didn't have an iPhone. (Must have left it at home by mistake.) He had to use cables and telegrams to set up his buys and sells.

If Darvas could make millions from trading with that much of a technological handicap, is the latest, greatest technology really important at all? Or is it just likely to distract you, over-stimulate you, lead you astray?

Here's Pete's story of how technology kept him from succeeding:

Pete's tale

"When I started I was too keen to have some shares – I felt that by not doing something I was missing out on possible gains.

"You cover it in your books but now I realise that I do much better when I don't sit looking at shares when I'm bored! Daytime TV is often a more sensible choice.

"I found that I overtraded on spread betting initially as there's no commission or stamp duty – I really had to be more reserved. Also I found I used spread betting with more of a gambling approach. Having the spread betting apps on my phone encouraged me to keep checking what had gone up and down.

"After a while I deleted them from my phone as it was too addictive."

I did note that when Pete came to a seminar he had his eyes firmly fixed on his iPhone. If you have unemotional stop-losses in place there shouldn't be any need to constantly check for small changes to a share price. Once out and about, enjoy what you are doing rather than checking your phone.

Using mobile devices constantly is very addictive and will definitely lead to overtrading: another no no. You can see how Pete got addicted. He did brilliantly by deleting the apps that were affecting him. It's a hard thing to come off an app, maybe even as hard as giving up smoking.

Sharks understand that being attached to a screen of any kind all day is a bad move. You are almost doomed to fail to achieve shark status. Instead of decluttering the mind you add even more clutter.

I went to a lovely restaurant last week, very expensive but great food. A young couple came in and sat at the next table. From the minute they sat down, their phones came out. They hardly exchanged a word between them while they Twittered and Facebooked, taking pictures of the food so that their online 'friends' could see it.

They weren't really there 'in the moment'. Their brains were too cluttered to enjoy just chatting to someone. The postings were showing off to people who weren't there and couldn't care less.

In effect, 'mobile phones' *aren't* – they are computers. Hardly anyone uses them as a phone. The couple had gone to dinner with the equivalent of their laptops open.

My wife and I went on a road trip abroad and part of it was to visit a relative. We looked forward to it, but the relative and his wife were so hooked on their phones that we could barely talk to them. We were sitting round a table but they had done the equivalent of getting out their laptops. Their kids did the same. We haven't communicated with them since.

Just as the 'phone' destroyed our real relationship so it can destroy your chance of trading properly. As can sitting on your computer all day.

Let me tell you a secret: I don't even own a mobile phone. I don't need an app or whatever to trade or do anything. I want to rest my mind and reboot whenever I can, not spend more time on a screen. If you want to contact me, ring the landline and I'll call you back when I'm ready...

Social media

Speaking of new technology, we need to talk in particular about social media: Twitter, Facebook, Instagram, bulletin boards, chat rooms, [insert any crazy new social media platform that has been created since this book came out here].

The more you look at all these things, the less like a shark you become.

Studies show that social media can effect the brain like cocaine. Researchers at California State University found technology-related addictions share neural features with gambling and substance addictions. Social sites stimulate the brain's amygdala and striatum, the same regions associated with compulsive behaviour. This can be disastrous for traders, who get a high from following others.

I have noticed several people addicted to social media in their answers to questionnaires I have sent out and in general correspondence.

One chap called Brian had lost a lot of money by getting tips from people on Twitter. He had become totally consumed by financial Twitter feeds. He'd spend all day on Twitter looking at what other people were doing and trying to copy them. It was the same with bulletin boards – he found himself trading like crazy trying to keep up.

He had a job as well as his trading and he realised his work was suffering. His bosses noticed too.

Thankfully, he realised his mistakes and fixed them. He stopped looking at any social media. He reduced his trading significantly. "It was really hard," he said. He had made nearly all his decisions based on what other people were doing and never did any of his own research. Now he tweets occasionally, but never anything to do with finance.

Someone else emailed me with an interesting comment:

"I do find myself immersed in Twitter feeds and at times feel good that someone else is making the same mistakes as me."

This is interesting, of course, in the sense of being deeply alarming! Good feelings from someone else getting it wrong? That's pretty cold comfort...

I think you will find being immersed in social media is never a good idea. I know it can be hard if you trade from home. It gives you the illusion of company. The problem is that social media isn't particularly honest company. I don't mean every post is a lie. But people who put themselves out there only tell you their best bits.

For example, on their Facebook pages people don't put a crap pic of themselves up there do they? They don't upload the selfies where they're blinking and there's food stuck in their teeth. And all the entries are amazing, darling. Here is the latest great meal I had. Look at this windsurfing I was doing! Check me out on holiday! Don't me and my partner look adorable...

You won't find any entries saying, "Had a row with my bastard of a boyfriend this morning, What a **** he is." Or "That was the worst holiday ever. And the kids drove me crazy. Couldn't wait to get home..."

Apart from the odd person who likes to commiserate with others' mistakes (see above), it will be exactly the same with those talking about their trades on social media. They will regale you with stories of their victories... but when it comes to bad losses? Those will be brushed under the carpet.

Those who broadcast a lot on social media also tend to be very strong personalities and that invariably means they are suffering from the problems with ego we looked at in chapter 10. There's no use in cutting out ego in your own trading if you're going to go and expose yourself to someone else's.

Social media also makes it too easy to play the blame game.

> *"It's not my fault I lost lots of money, it's that sod on Twitter! And all those sods on the bulletin boards. That sodding guy in that magazine – and that other total sod, Robbie Burns!"*

I have heard from a number of people who find it hard to concentrate on trading, not only from social media but also from email overload. Emails can bombard people and lead to stress and feeling overwhelmed. Another reason why the latest technology going off in your pocket every ten seconds may not be a great idea for a trader.

How to beat the overload

If you have been using social media it can be very hard to quit looking at what others are doing. And most of us have been using email for, blimey – decades.

One of Twitter's co-founders, Evan Williams, has called for an app that liberates people from incessant updates by delivering emails in a single batch each day. He also said that Twitter itself had been overwhelmed by the volume of posts. The company is increasingly experimenting with ways to help average users digest the never-ending torrent of new Tweets arriving in their streams.

Traders even ten years ago just wouldn't have had all this to deal with – I suspect it made them better traders.

In the absence of any great invention to solve this problem for us all, here's my suggestion for social media/email overload.

Unless obviously essential for your work, **do not look at emails or social media between the hours of 8am–4.30pm (while the UK market is open)**. At 4.30pm relax, have a cup of tea, put some distance between yourself and the market – and at 5pm, look at emails and social media (if you want to).

You'll find you'll be in a much more relaxed frame of mind. You can look at Twitter, Facebook or whatever and see what people have been saying. But you won't get caught up at 10am with someone saying "I bought this, you should too, it's greeeaaat!".

Just because a social media account or website looks lovely and professional doesn't mean the writer at the other end knows anything at all. You might be getting influenced by a 16-year-old writing in-between lessons for all you know.

You may find this quite hard to do at first. Checking social media is seriously habit-forming. But I bet you know in your heart of hearts that these influences stop you from being a shark during trading hours.

Sharks make their own decisions. They don't need to know what everyone else is up to.

Spread Betting and CFDs

Once upon a time you could actually telephone your spread betting broker to put on a trade. Maybe you still can. But spread betting and CFDs are very much a digital beast if you ask me – all those flashing buttons, all those instant updates.

A trading shark knows the big advantages of spread betting. As mentioned in passing elsewhere in the book it's a great tool, especially as you can make money when the market is going down.

But in the wrong hands it can be a total disaster. People ask me: why not just spread bet instead of trading in an ISA or other broker account? The answer is: because you would need the ultimate brain to avoid destroying yourself.

Spread betting is a great tool but should *only* be used alongside trading in a normal self-select ISA.

In a normal account you don't see stuff going up and down every second – or lots of lovely flashing buttons shouting at you: "Trade, trade – go on you know you want to!"

Look at any spread betting company and the most popular traded things are things nearly everyone loses on: currencies, gold, oil, Apple, indices. All highly volatile markets.

It is all down to the brain wanting quick money. Go on – 'pep things up a bit'. Lose £100,000. It'll be an afternoon to remember!

Even the losses are a little bit thrilling in spread betting. Then there is all the fun of trying to make those losses back. But you must know where it all ends.

So a shark thinks: spread betting is great, I can use it when I don't have any more allowable money to put into my ISA, but I won't overuse the leverage and I won't be tempted to overtrade, play with things I don't understand or use it for boredom trading.

Spread betting done right can work very much in a shark's favour. Ordinary stop-losses, for example, don't work if a share already opens up well down after a profit warning before the market opens. But with spread betting there is a **guaranteed stop** whereby you know for sure how much you will lose on a trade. You can't do this in a normal account.

I cover more about spread betting in depth in my other two books, especially *The Naked Trader's Guide to Spread Betting* (you could probably tell that from the title).

Technical Gibberish and Jargon

If you're going to be a success you must have a clear head. Mr Spock logically eradicates everything from his brain that isn't necessary. So does a shark. If your brain is full of stuff you won't concentrate on the basics. (The basics make you money.) You'll get confused as hell.

One of the biggest sources of useless, brain-cluttering 'stuff' for traders is technical gibberish and jargon. (Yes, that's the technical name.)

"When you are confused, it is best to do nothing. You are just going for a random walk and that is when you are liable to get mugged, because you don't have staying power. You are likely to be faked out by some stray fluctuations because you lack the courage of your convictions. As my friend, Victor Niederhoffer says, the market destroys the weak – that is, investors who don't have well founded convictions. You need some convictions to avoid getting faked out, but having the courage of your convictions could get you wiped out if your convictions are false. So, I prefer to take a stand only when I have well-founded convictions."

George Soros

Getting technical

The problem new traders face when they start out is the temptation to try too hard – and that leads to them getting technical. They buy books, go to seminars and read stuff riddled with jargon. Their heads get full of systems, indications, screens, charts, lines...

Here's an example of a correspondent in the most recent edition of *The Naked Trader* whose head had been crammed with gibberish:

"I have been placing buy orders just above the first bullish candlestick after a pullback on the weekly chart, provided the 10 weekly MA is above the 20 MA, and this is above the 50 MA, when the MACD is rising on the monthly chart."

This carries on at greater length but you get the drift.

The rest of his email explained that he had spent over £5,000 on DVDs, courses and textbooks. He didn't need to spend any of that. All that was required was a clear brain, not one packed full of nonsense.

Training courses

Going by what attendees have told me, many training courses out there that swamp people with technical analysis and other jargon are run by those on the make. The instructors don't really know what they are doing and use gibberish and jargon to try and make it look as if it is very complicated and they are guiding you through it.

So, frankly, I feel most trading seminars are a total rip-off. I know this sounds a bit rich from someone like me who runs six or so every year. But I do believe mine give genuine guidance – and they are run by someone who *has* made more than a million from smallish money.

I also know from those who have attended rip-off ones that they are keen to sell all kinds of trading systems to attendees – more stuff they can charge you for. Some also love charging for 'ongoing support'.

These don't teach you how to be a shark at all.

Don't go on any course unless you are certain the person running it has really made a lot of money – slowly and legitimately. Otherwise you will end up with a young guy in a Primark suit giving you a load of baloney that some Mr Big Boss has taught him to recite.

Riding high in the charts

Charts have been the downfall of many. For some reason, traders start thinking that a chart can tell them everything they need to know about a share. "It's all there!", "I don't even care what the company makes!", "I'm not even sure I'm bothered how you spell the company's name!"

"The essential element is that the markets are ultimately based on human psychology, and by charting the markets you're merely converting human psychology into graphic representations. I believe that the human mind is more powerful than any computer in analyzing the implications of this graph."
Al Weiss

At least people who rely on charts have some kind of a plan. It's better than nothing. But a shark knows you can't possibly rely on one thing *alone* to decide a trade.

After all, we are in a business. If you owned a café you wouldn't just choose one supplier when you go shopping – you'd look at a lot of suppliers to make the right business decision.

And you wouldn't buy a load of coffee beans or iced buns without trying them – or even knowing that they were coffee beans or iced buns – just because on paper you saw you could put a big mark-up on them.

Trying to use charts alone doesn't work. Only one aspect of a share – price movement – is looked at. However, non-sharks love it. They think that they are being unemotional, cool and calculating. But they are simply looking at one part of the story. If a trade is a jigsaw puzzle they have a lot of pieces missing.

And often they actually *are* being emotional: because technical analysis feels 'cool'. It has its special language. It comes with expensive software packages. There are lots of gurus about. It appeals to the ego.

Here's Phil, who thought it was the answer:

> "I used to only use charts for everything and filled them with moving averages, MACD, Stochastics etc. You name it and I had it! I even moved to Ichimoko charts as they had more colours. I ended up losing on virtually every trade I placed. Now I just look at charts to see an up or down trend – the only other thing is to try and see support and resistance levels."

In the end, thank Spock, Phil saw that charts on their own don't cut it. There is no problem at all in having a look at them as part of an *overall* picture. Sharks and Vulcans do. It's just that they know you can't use one aspect of anything to make a proper business decision.

What's needed vs what isn't

So, when it comes to technical stuff, you don't need most of it. But you might need some of it.

What is what?

You do not need:

- a trading system

- a charting package

- a DVD boxset about technical analysis

- tickets to a rip-off seminar.

You do need:

- real-time prices

- maybe Level 2

- share screens (a way of screening shares by certain categories: those breaking out to the upside, say. Not massive screens with share prices on!).

The above shouldn't cost too much. You can get them from sites like ADVFN or its competitors. I explain how to use them in depth in *The Naked Trader*.

Share screens are a good technical way of finding ideas for future trades. But you don't need to rely on technical stuff for even that. Other places to get ideas include:

- Stockopedia (a great source of Vulcan-like facts and figures – it even has stock screens based on my book. They offer a discount here: **www.stockopedia.com/nakedtrader**)

- specialist magazines like *MoneyWeek*, *Investors Chronicle* and *Shares*

- national newspaper City pages.

(Remember you are looking for ideas not tips.)

Sharks Can Lose It

I'm obviously hoping this book will make you more cool and calculating in your trading but even with the best will in the world sharks or Vulcans can for one reason or another lose the plot from time to time.

Even Mr Spock lost his cool, most memorably when he was on a planet which had some dodgy drug plants. One naughty sniff and you're drugged up. Old Spock went nuts and even did bad things with a woman he'd only just met.

Losing the plot

If you find that for six months you manage the cool calculating thing, but then things start to slip, you need to crackdown on it right away. Try and figure out what the problem is. Use this book. I wrote it for you.

Maybe you've started to ignore stop-losses. Or got lazy checking your research. Or given into one of the eight deadly emotions. Your previous discipline has disappeared.

You must urgently do some self-assessment (not the tax kind). Have a cold hard look. Has something happened in your life that has annoyed you, changed your mood?

Are you in need of some excitement? Is it a mid-life crisis? Are you comfort trading? Bored?

Quiz yourself and figure out what it is. Check the trades that went wrong and write down why they did. Once you know, go back to basics. If you struggle to fix it, don't make any trades till you have conquered it.

"For the past eight years I have been working with top-notch Wall Street traders unearthing specific psychological issues that interfere with the trading process. These include resistance, fear of failure, defensive behaviour, negative self-characterizations, and negative mindsets that become self-fulfilling prophesies."

Ari Kiev

Let's say you had a big row with a loved one, or things aren't going well in a relationship. Are you starting to lose it in your trading because you're losing it in your emotional life?

In a standard business it doesn't much matter if one or two people in that business are going through a hard time in their personal lives – there are other people there to stop bad decisions being made. You can't overdo it, over-order stock, run riot – you'll get stopped by others or your bosses.

But in trading *you* are the boss. If you go off the rails because of problems in your personal life, there is nothing to stop you. If you have a row with your partner and start overtrading, no one will stand in your way. If you finish the box set of *Game of Thrones* and suddenly feel as manly as Charles Dance, no one can prevent you sticking on a hundred reckless trades that will all lose.

Except for you.

If you feel your life outside trading is getting you down in any way or making you feel heightened emotions, let me offer the best solution: STOP!

Don't buy anything at all until the rough patch you are experiencing has run its course. Put stops (preferably trailing stops) on all the trades you have open at sensible places so your pre-existing trades can run their conclusion to bigger profits or small losses.

By doing this, all the bad feelings you are having won't affect your trading as much.

I think part of the reason for trading problems appearing alongside emotional problems is that emotional problems can lead to self-destructive urges – 'screw everything' feelings (I didn't mean screw everything literally, ahem).

Even the best-grounded people can be affected by events out of their control.

Taking timeouts

Our poor old minds are chock-a-block with stuff. Do I need to do some shopping? What's for dinner? Is that ache I have some kind of illness? Should I sell some shares? What's on TV tonight? Does that mum on the school run hate me or not?

You see what I'm getting at.

The more cluttered we are, the less likely we are to be clear-headed when it comes to making a trade. It's true of ordinary days as much as volatile days – though the latter can certainly be worse.

Something you should therefore do most days as a trader is declutter. Take a timeout. (Dip it in a cup of tea. Beautiful!)

The idea is to switch off your brain for a bit. Just like you need to switch off your computer when it has been running lots of programs for ages.

"Fatigue and mental overload create a loss of concentration – the demands of watching the screen hour after hour make it difficult to be sharp, creating fatigue effects that are well-known to pilots, car drivers, and soldiers."

Brett Steenbarger

So here are a few ideas on how to take trading timeouts. Maybe one will suit you, maybe not – see if you can come up with your own ones too.

- Gym/swim. Swimming is my favourite timeout. If I find my head is exploding I love having a relaxing swim. I do it most days actually. There's the gym too – go and have a crosstrain or lift some weights you alpha male dude.

- Read a chapter of fiction. Grab a crap book (Hey, not *this* one!). I'm in the middle of writing a novel right now, so maybe give that one a go...

- Write a list. Get an old-fashioned pen and some paper and write a list of stuff you have to do that is bugging you. Car MOT, a laptop to fix, shopping to do – whatever it is, get it down along with ideas of when you might do it.

- Play a game. Make sure it isn't computer-based. (You want to get away from screens for a bit.) Chess? Cards? Take the dog out?

- Walk – out you go! Have a walk, even just round the neighbourhood. Do *not* take a phone with you.

- Watch some crap TV. As long as it isn't Doomberg, go for it! *Deal or No Deal, Cash in the Attic* (that's what you'll wish you had done instead of trading shares). I watch loads of crap.

You should find that when you get back to your trading screen you feel a lot better. To borrow a phrase from up North (and so patronise any Northern readers):

"If in doubt do nowt".

The importance of sex

Hormones are often responsible for traders losing it if they're men (sorry lads). They lie behind some of the most risky stock market behaviour, as this *BBC* article reports:

Both cortisol and testosterone occur naturally in the body. Levels of cortisol increase when we experience psychological or physical stress. This causes the blood sugar levels to rise and prepares the body for a fight or flight response.

High testosterone levels in men have been shown to make them confident and successful in competitive situations. [Of course, the confidence is often misplaced! – Robbie]

Previous research has shown that male traders make significantly higher profits on days when their morning testosterone levels are above their daily average.

Writing in *Scientific Reports*. the authors carried out two experiments as part of their study.

First, they measured natural levels of the two hormones in 142 male and female volunteers while they played a trading game in groups of ten.

Men who had higher levels of cortisol were more likely to take risks, which led to instability in prices.

But there did not appear to be a link between cortisol and risky trading in the women who took part, which is consistent with other research showing that women respond to stress in different ways.

In a second experiment, 75 young men were given one of the hormones before playing the game, and then a placebo.

The results showed that cortisol appeared to encourage riskier investments, while testosterone increased the feeling that they were on a winning streak.

The research team said their work gave a better understanding of traders' behaviour and how it might affect financial markets.

Dr Ed Roberts, study author from the department of medicine at Imperial College London, said the traders' working environment was key: "They are like elite athletes – they need to be looked after."

He also said there was more research to do.

"We only looked at the acute effects of the hormones in the lab. It would be interesting to measure traders' hormone levels in the real world, and also to see what the longer-term effects might be."

Dr Richard Quinton, consultant and senior lecturer in endocrinology at Newcastle-upon-Tyne Hospitals and University, said it looked to be a "powerful and robust study".

He added that an obvious area for future research would be looking at the behavioural effects of giving small doses of cortisol inhibitors to traders.

Prof Ashley Grossman, professor of endocrinology at the University of Oxford, said the study suggested that raised hormone levels can both cause instability in the stock markets and feed off it.

"The male ego – that wonderful trait that has been bringing us wars, riots, and bloodshed since time immemorial – tends to get heavily caught up in trading. A guy studies his charts, decides to buy, and now his self-esteem is involved – he has to be right! If the market goes his way, he waits to be proven even more right – bigger is better. If the market goes against him, he is tough enough to stand the pain, and waits for the market to reverse and prove him right – while it grinds down his account."

Alexander Elder

I know that 90% of the readers of this book will be male. Over the years, only around 10% of traders at my seminars have been women. If 50 come to a seminar I know only five or six will be female. Broader market statistics bear this out.

And guess what, ego-fuelled men reading this (yes, YOU!), women tend to make better traders and investors.

Above all this is because women are more likely to let losing trades go. This is perhaps not a surprise as they tend to be better at cutting a relationship that's a bit of a loser. (I have been on the end of that!)

Women traders tell me they just can't cope with the thought of something running into a big loss. Generally if I'm in a room of traders and ask "Who is holding a trade with a loss of more than 25%?" you can guarantee most of the men put their hands up. The women? Rarely.

However – and here is where I can stick up for the blokes – men *do* tend to be better at letting profits run than women. Men seem to enjoy the delayed gratification of waiting for the profits to build.

Here is top trader Alexander Elder with his thoughts on women traders:

"Women traders are much more likely to ask a simple question: Where's the money? They like to take profits and avoid losses instead of trying to prove themselves right. Women are more likely to bend with the wind and go with the flow, catch trends, and hop off a little earlier, booking profits.

"When I tell traders that keeping records is a hugely important aspect of success, women are more likely to keep them than men. If you are looking to hire a trader, all other factors being equal, I'd recommend looking for a woman."

Dr Elder (he sounds a bit scary so I'll keep it formal) confirms my view that women are excellent loss takers, though they could try and run the profits further.

He also points out that women are much better at keeping records, which helps their success too. That's true: one of the best female traders I know keeps immaculate records. She knows all her buy and sell points, stops, she even keeps track of her performances using a chart she calls her "equity curve".

(She also goes to meetings with CEOs and only buys if their shoes have been carefully looked after and fully buffed.)

She finds all that very helpful. Personally I struggle with that kind of thing.

Fiona shared her thoughts earlier on how to conquer fear. She has some excellent insight into the advantages and disadvantages of sex as a trader:

"We women like a stash of cash for a rainy day. Nothing like a good hoard to cheer me up. Generally that really helps me get out of trades early because I tend to use tight stops and I don't have too much of a problem taking a loss.

"Letting profits run is another matter and here I still struggle. Honestly I think it requires a much bigger psychological shift than learning to cut and run. There is a great temptation once a share is slightly in profit to take the money and clear off to the nearest shoe shop. The problem is you end up forever trading and never making serious money.

"Taking a loss, though hard, opens a script in my head which is about getting it wrong, being rubbish at stock picking, doing badly while everyone else is coining it and so on. Though painful, it is familiar and therefore I am biased towards it – a lovely bit of self-sabotage if ever there was one. I bet a lot of other people are the same.

"Letting profits run is about delayed gratification, being bold and maybe being successful – stepping into a brave new world. That's a very different script to have running in your head and I feel really uncomfortable with it. I haven't mastered it yet."

As traders we have to marry the two: men and women's best bits in a lovely marriage – cut the loss, run the profit.

From Non-shark to Shark

"It's hard, it's hard. It's hard out here for a (shark – Ed.)"

It's not easy to trade like a shark – you only have to look at the statistics. Most traders are confirmed Kirks. Why is it so hard for so many to make money by modelling themselves on Mr Spock?

I think Jason Zweig, author of *Your Money and Your Brain*, explains it well:

> "Emotional circuits deep within our brain make us crave whatever is likely to be rewarding and shun whatever is liable to be risky. To counteract these impulses from cells that originally developed tens of millions of years ago, your brain only has a thin veneer of relatively modern analytical circuits that are often no match for the blunt emotional power of the most ancient part of your mind.

That is why knowing the right answer and doing the right thing are very different."

So it is the oldest part of our caveman brain that stops us from winning in the markets! The blunt power of years ago defeats the new. Or, to put it another way, the weapon a caveman used to bang an animal over the head with defeats the latest iPad app.

As you make the transition to trading like Mr Spock, here are the caveman ways that might get in the way – and how to overcome them. I'll also share my own struggles.

Repeating mistakes

It's very human to repeat mistakes. It is what lots of traders do. They keep making the very same mistake and not learning from it. Time and time again.

It's very human to repeat mistakes. It is what lots of traders do. They keep—

Er, sorry! But it is so very easy to do...

I was coaching a kids football team and we had a brilliant goalie – he always made tons of great saves. But he had one flaw: instead of rolling it out to the defence so we had possession, he kicked it to the other end of the pitch where our young attackers were too small to get it. So it ended up pretty much straight away back in the possession of the rival team.

I would say at the beginning of the game: "Don't kick it out. Kick or roll it gently to one of our defence so we can begin a move. Every time you kick it to the other end of the pitch the other team end up in control."

And he could manage this for a bit. But after a while he couldn't help himself. In the heat of the game, he started to kick the ball far away again.

It was the same in one episode of *Star Trek* – the humans were stuck in a time loop always making the same mistake, which ended with the ship blowing up. After the ship exploded, the loop restarted – but the same result always followed. Kaboom.

In the end it was the ship's robot that realised the same mistake was being made and put it right, saving the ship.

Many traders confess to me that they keep repeating the same pattern of behaviour even if they lose money as a result. It could be anything: not using stop-losses, relying too much on technical analysis, bagging a profit way too early and never allowing the good gains to happen.

The first step is to identify the mistake. Because you're on the path to sharkdom, the good thing is that this should be easier now. In fact, you probably already have a good idea. If not, don the pointy ears and examine what you've been doing. Look at your records. Find the pattern. Is it over-trading, succumbing to the excitement of gambling, failing to do research, buying or selling too soon?

Whatever it is, owning up to it is the first and most important step in changing that behaviour. Take the emotion out of it – don't feel bad, just face up to it. Then follow the tips I've outlined in this book for the specific issue.

Not using stop-losses or letting your wins run? It's probably because you haven't got a proper trading plan: get one and stick to it (run your trading like a business!). Using too much leverage? Putting on too many trades? You're looking for excitement. Set aside 5% of your total funds in a totally separate account and go bananas with just that money (no leverage, no top ups from your funds, that's it). And so on.

Sometimes people tell me they manage to stop repeating mistakes but after six months or a year or two, the issue resurfaces. It seems to be very difficult indeed to cut out our favourite mistakes for good. It's like when my dentist finishes putting in a load of new fillings.

In a treatment plan note he'll also say something along the lines of, "Just because those three teeth are filled doesn't mean this is the end of the story, if you carry on eating Twixes and not brushing and flossing properly you will be back for more and soon."

Just because you think you have fixed a trading mistake doesn't mean it won't come right back at ya. Just stick to the process above – take action! – and don't despair. Despair would be emotional and the best traders are not emotional.

When people don't change

I'd like to tell you about one of the most frustrating but fascinating things I have come across as a trader working with thousands of other traders. It's the strange phenomenon of people who read my trading book, perhaps even come to a seminar, and despite understanding what I'm saying and agreeing with it, can't stop themselves from doing the *exact* opposite of what I suggest.

I hope that doesn't sound egotistical – it's just that I didn't use to understand it. Why would someone agree with me and sometimes spend a whole day with me and yet not take any of it on board?

I can say, "Have a trading plan" till I'm blue in the face but they will still bung on a trade because someone on Twitter did. I can say, "Don't trade penny shares, don't trade emotionally, don't put all your eggs in one basket, ignore social media" and yet some will still get excited about concentrating their entire portfolio into one tiny share they heard about on Facebook.

It is simply psychology. It's in their make-up. And it is very hard for them to fix.

I used to feel a bit cross about it, thinking 'Why oh why did they do it?', 'What the hell?' and lots of bad words I can't use here. I really want people to succeed at trading. Why read me and then do the opposite?

But more recently (perhaps the wisdom of age?), I relax about it. People are people, humans are humans – we all make mistakes all the time. I can't expect everyone to immediately get the shark way. Some will read my stuff and think, 'Yeah, that makes sense' but carry on their self-destructive way.

Maybe it is the same as having counselling. The counsellor sensibly tells you what is going wrong in your life – and you agree with the counsellor but still can't help but screw up. Or you know you are an alcoholic or a gambler and you can't help but continue to drink and gamble even though you know you shouldn't.

I realise I can only try and guide you a bit with the trading – the good news is I have had enough feedback to know that people can change even though initially it looks hopeless.

Realism vs fantasy

As you become cooler and more logical, running your trading as a business, you should start to see the benefits. Profits ought to be up. That portfolio ought to be looking pretty good.

It's at that point that some traders get carried away and stop being realistic about what gains are achievable.

This is also something that afflicts traders just starting out. I can't even count the number of people who have emailed me in the past wanting to be full-time traders, expecting a decent full-time income – with only £20,000 in capital to do it.

I say to them: "If you can live off £5,000 a year, then fine, you can do it."

Decent traders can expect to make 20–25% on their capital per year. Given that the market won't make that as a whole most years, it's a pretty big profit. Some would even say it's ambitious and 10% may be more realistic. Did you know that if you make 7.2% a year and let it compound you will double your money every ten years? So there are plenty of acceptable targets anywhere between 10–25%.

Don't get carried away wanting more.

Watching too many TV shows or movies about traders is often the culprit here. So is social media, which tends to be full of people bragging about how much they have made, or people trying to con you with systems promising ludicrous returns. Also, ego can come into it – thinking our ability is greater than it is. Or simply being in a dreamland, thinking how nice it would be to 'work from home and trade'.

You must stay realistic. There is no problem at all with trading with smaller amounts and nothing wrong with starting to trade with £5,000 or so. But don't expect to give up the day job anytime soon. Congratulate yourself with gains of 10–25% on whatever sum you have available.

My struggles

While I think most of the time I maintain shark status I am actually human and can be tempted into non-shark behaviour as much as anyone else.

Let me tell you some of my ongoing weak points. As you read them, join in by having a think about what yours might be. It'll be just like a counselling session but free – except for whatever you paid for the book (if you illegally downloaded it then you're not allowed to join in).

Even though I wrote this book and I feel I know a lot about trading psychology it doesn't mean I find it easy myself to maintain the shark approach!

- When the market is motoring down I am quick to short the FTSE but I am not so good at banking the profits on this quickly enough. I have to work harder on getting stops in the right place.

- I find it very easy to love a share or company. Sometimes I buy too much of a share and hold it for too long.

- My work area can get messy and I know it affects me.

- I probably spread bet a bit too much and for too much and sometimes it affects my mood. I have to bank profits more often and tuck them away to stop the temptation to overtrade.

- I am a bit too keen on 'jam tomorrow' stories, i.e. companies with a great story to tell. Maybe it's because I was a journalist. I love a good story!

Story-telling trouble

One story I really liked was that of a company which had technology that could suss out if a driver was too tired to drive. I could see the huge potential for lorry companies and so on. I became very keen on the shares and bought loads thinking it was going to be huge.

But I was blindsided and had fallen into confirmation bias. I didn't look at the cold hard figures. I thought, "It won't be long before they win a major contract and I'll be in the money!" In fact, it wasn't long before... absolutely nothing happened.

It wasn't too bad – the shares just went down a bit. But I was in them for two years – an utter waste of time, and I could have used the money in much better trades.

I think I have beaten this last weakness. How? First I look at the cold hard figures. How much is it making now? Not much? How much cash has it got now? Not much? And how much does the market think it is worth now? HOW MUCH!!!!?

If I like the story but it's not a good time to buy, I add it to a watchlist. It helps scratch the itch to be active and allows me to keep a vague eye on it and see if things change in future.

Averaging down to doom

Another weakness of mine used to be averaging down – buying more of a losing share in my portfolio. I have definitely cracked that for good, though! It doesn't matter how tempted I get, I never do it.

How did I crack it? By incorporating stop-losses into all my trading plans. I am out of a bad trade before it goes down enough for me to even think about averaging down.

Maybe the share is even more attractive lower – well, that's fine, but I can wait and see what happens before buying back in, rather than leaving all my money tied up in it and dependent on things turning round. (Funny how that skews one's ability to be logical.)

Those are my confessions – what are yours? Write them down, it may help!

People can change

I have discussed a lot of people's screw-ups in this book. And while it's true that some people are very unlikely to change, many of us can. Let's close this chapter with some encouraging examples of what we're all trying to do: be more like cold-hearted businessmen from another planet.

Andy's tale

Andy managed to become a Vulcan. Spock-like, he cleared out his crap and started again.

> "I have cleared my account of all of my positions. After using your analysis and selection techniques I realised they weren't high quality stocks. I then went long on high quality stocks, using proper stops and targets.

> "I am very pleased to report that in only four weeks my account is up 9.3%.

"On reflection, the biggest difference (not including the account balance) is rather more intangible, and that's my confidence in trading has increased so much due to a better understanding of the markets, and the gift that is Level 2!"

Ed's tale

Here's a story from Ed who also succeeded in making major changes to his trading:

"In the years before the dotcom bubble burst, I worked for a certain technology company. We were all encouraged to invest in our company through sharesave plans.

"As was typical at the time, the company's share price rose almost every day. I still vividly remember each morning switching on the office TV and selecting Teletext so we could monitor the share price – and discuss how much profit we'd get from our sharesave schemes.

"When my first sharesave plan matured, it bought us a family holiday in Cyprus.

"As the share price continued to go up, my healthy annual bonus went straight into buying more shares at their peak price of £5.50.

"Eventually the share price began to fall. But rather than see any danger, most of us considered it a great bargain and bought even more shares. Digging into savings, I bought more and more at various prices on the way down.

"After all, 60 pence had to be a bargain compared to the £5.50 it had reached just a few months before. And 34 pence was even better.

"But, eventually, when the share price reached the murky depths of £0.005 (yes, half a penny), the company did a debt for equity swap with the banks, thus weakening the share price even more.

"And that's where it stayed. I'd lost the whole lot. That's when I decided shares were a loser's game, and stayed clear for a long, long, time.

"Many years later, a conversation with a friend got me to think about reading how the experts actually made money from shares. So I bought a number of books, including the first edition of *The Naked Trader*, and eagerly digested them.

"That's when I realised I'd been doing everything wrong: buying shares on the way down; not looking at the company's fundamentals... From the books, I learned how to research and invest wisely. Dozens of A4 pages of notes later, I bought my first shares as a much more educated investor.

"But the share price hit the stop-loss and sold!

"To me, though, this was great! I'd been reading a bit about the psychology of trading. This time I was actually happy to lose a bit of money rather than watch it all waste away. I'd found a way to protect my cash.

"I went on to pick many winners, and continued to learn along the way.

"Now, years along the road, I still research every company I buy into, and I'm still more than happy to take small losses rather than watch the share price go down.

"And I still have a worthless share certificate to remind me of those crazy days."

It's a nice idea to keep that souvenir of past trading mistakes. It helps remind him that it is possible to change.

Ollie's tale

Ollie knew he was screwing up but realised he could fix it – and did:

"I got very lucky on my first ever trade (a penny share tip). I managed to get on it very low and it went really high. I thought there was nothing to this stock investing lark.

"When my friend's next tip came through, I backed it heavily (£10,000). I thought it had to be another good one and did not take precautions or have a plan. It dropped. I held it for 18 months with a constant up one penny, down one penny kind of action. After I started to read *The Naked Trader* I immediately dumped it. In fact, I dumped all of my 'tips' that I had bought without research. I held no stock.

"I kept reading the book… but unfortunately, despite initially learning from it, I somehow became the kind of person who does the exact opposite of what you say to do. I got to the spread betting chapter and immediately opened an account with £1,300. I then played it for a day. I used very small amounts and made a number of mistakes at first but by reading the book and trying things out I did at least understand how a spread betting account works.

"I am writing this now at the end of trading a few days later. I have just taken all my money out of my account. It was £1,109 at the end. It got up to £1,560 at one point and down to £1,000 at another. During two days trading (and over the weekend in-between) I could think of nothing else but trading. What if I miss a trade? I was using jumping straight into them with no research. In the two days that I traded I made 55 trades!

"I have realised that I am not the right person at all for spread betting. All the things you mention I could see in myself. I am obsessive, excitable and moody. I spent all day at my desk doing no work and watching a screen go blue and red. I started off trading low and as I got better increased the stakes. I was not a nice person and had no time for anyone or anything but trading.

"On the plus side, I have found that I am not afraid of taking a loss as I always put stops and trailing stops on every bet. It could have been a lot worse.

"I have come out losing about £200. I think of this as the price I have paid for 'a live and hands-on seminar' that has proved that spread betting is not for me.

"So, having never made a penny on the stock markets (all my trades and investments add up to a net loss), I still think that by following your advice in your book there is money to be made, especially in an ISA and SIPP.

"I am in a good financial position with a lot of disposable income and two properties that are rented out. And life is good. I think that I need blue chips because of my character and nature."

This is very interesting from Ollie. He admits he did the opposite of everything I said he should do when it comes to spread betting. His emotions took charge. Trading brought out the Captain Kirk in him. He even started disliking himself; his crazed bout of trading turned him into a person who cared about nothing but the screen.

But he realised the problem fast. He stopped. And before he had made any major losses. Now he talks about ISAs and blue chips. He's toyed with the devil and realises he has to stop. He can take a loss, which is brilliant, so there is definitely a future in trading for him.

If there is one message from this book it is: **know your own faults and take appropriate steps to limit their impact on your trading**. For some that might mean not trading at all, or not trading for some time, for most of us it means taking less drastic but not less definite measures.

"To be a successful trader, you have to be able to admit mistakes. People who are very bright don't make very many mistakes. In a sense, they generally are correct. In trading, however, the person who can easily admit to being wrong is the one who walks away a winner. Besides trading, there is probably no other profession where you have to admit you're wrong. In trading, you can't hide your failures. Your equity provides a daily reflection of your performance. The trader who tries to blame his losses on external events will never learn from his mistakes. For a trader, rationalization is a guaranteed road to ultimate failure."

Victor Sperandeo

Dear Mr Spock Problem Page

Mr Spock is here to answer your problems. Every trader needs a green-blooded Agony Aunt in their life... Luckily people who trade like sharks are a tight-knit community and I was able to impose upon the good Commander to help my readers out.[3]

Where to work?

Dear Mr Spock,

What are your thoughts on working environment? Does it really affect quality of trading or is it a red herring?

Being an office worker I am used to a desk and an office chair. My options at home are: a comfy armchair with a laptop (with the possible addition of a cat who likes to drape himself across the keyboard), or the kitchen table and a hard wooden chair.

Jane

---

3   Legally I am obliged to point out this is a lie. Sorry.

Dear Jane,

I must be tough with you. Logically, if you sit in an armchair with the cat over the keyboard you won't get much done. A comfy chair means being able to take short naps. Short naps can end up as longer naps. Comfy chairs are also invariably aimed at televisions, or near to piles of books and magazines.

Also, the cat might press a sell or buy button by accident and nowhere in the known universe are cats renowned for their prowess at trading shares.

Though it sounds uncomfortable, you are much better off trading on the hard wooden chair at the kitchen table. Then you can visit the armchair when you want to relax and have a break.

"Environmental distractions and boredom cause a lack of focus – all of us have limits to our attention span and these are easily taxed during quiet times in the market."

Brett Steenbarger

How can I cure my fatal flaw?

Dear Mr Spock,

I am still trying to identify what makes a successful trader so that I can leave the tedious day job.

I find it nearly impossible to act on my stop-losses – I can never tell whether the market won't just turn tomorrow. Is this a fatal flaw in my trading and if so is there a cure?

Alan

Dear Alan,

First, make sure you have enough capital to leave that tedious day job. Sorry to be a BOFV (Boring Old Fart Vulcan).

Next, I find it totally illogical that you cannot 'act' on your stop-losses. Don't you want to them to, well, stop your losses? You must place the stops with your broker or spread bet firm to ensure they are carried out regardless of your emotions.

If you find you cannot do this, you can never join us on Planet Vulcan.

Portfolio size worry

Dear Mr Spock,

I am very worried in that I think mine is too small. I would like to make it bigger if I could. Do you think I could make it bigger?

Jeff

Dear Jeff,

I have a big one myself but like you I used to have a small one. But do not worry – a small one can grow into a big one naturally with some effort and application.

Having a small portfolio can actually be easier – one can nip in and out of shares. But understand it can take time to achieve a big one like me. Be patient, make good Vulcan trades – or shark trades, if you insist; as they say on earth, from little acorns great oaks can grow.

Room for improvement

Dear Mr Spock,

Unfortunately, I lost a lot of money investing in small oil companies. I was convinced at least one of them would make a major find but I have been very disappointed in them all. I still hold most of them. What do you think I could do to improve my trading?

Simon

Dear Simon,

You wrote to me wanting a Vulcan take on things but you won't like my answer.

That said, I have to be unemotional about your silly human need to be told everything will be OK.

It won't.

You haven't been trading but gambling. And indeed being greedy, thinking you were going to make millions from terrible trades. You appear not to have made one sensible business-like trade.

Your only hope of becoming a Vulcan is to sell all your rubbish immediately. Take your remaining capital and start again, preferably after a break. Treat every trade properly from a business point of view with exit plans and real research.

I am afraid your chances of making it are low, but not impossible. If you try one more time but find yourself breaking into the same bad habits, find some other way to lose money.

A total banker

Dear Mr Spock,

I bought a lot of shares in a bank. I couldn't help myself, they looked so cheap. But I've lost £33,000 in them. I've had to borrow quite a lot of money to cover the loss and I am still paying that off. I bought two other bank shares six months ago as they were both rising but I'm now in a big loss with those too. I also lost £6,000 on the FTSE recently as I thought it was going to go up. I am in a bit of a mess but I do love trading.

James

Dear James,

Stop. Now. Cut everything. Give up trading. Pay off the loan and move on. I think there is a 0% chance of you becoming a Vulcan.

There are too many problems here. You can't take a loss. You also said, "I love trading" – despite losing so much money. This is all too emotional.

I can only foresee more money being lost. Perhaps next you will try to make your money back on these shares by trading them still more. Get the pain over with now.

CONCLUSION

Well done, you just read *Trade Like a Shark*. Or skimmed it for the best bits more like...

I've tried to paint a picture for you of what it takes to be a psychologically successful trader: the overall mental framework you need (part I), the dangers of emotions (part II), and the traps that lie outside the mind but can nevertheless sabotage its workings (part III).

And I didn't tell you to think outside the box once.

You should now be well-armed to approach your trading in the best possible way: not like Leonardo DiCaprio snorting drugs off a laptop but like Mr Spock doing a crossword puzzle. Or like a cold-hearted great white patiently eating his way through the frightened little fishes and synchronised swimming teams of the rest of the market.

Of course, real life isn't perfect. It doesn't matter how much you try and have a perfect mind for trading, we can all go off the rails. I do myself from time to time, and perhaps part of the reason for writing this book is to be able to look at it when emotion takes over and think: 'Be like Spock. Cut that loser!' or 'Trade like a shark not a minnow!'

A reader of mine once wrote to me and said:

> "We all know we should have our trading rules and our trading plan. But if we were all goody two-shoes the whole time, how many of us would have got into this nefarious trading lark in the first place?"

This is very true. Because you bought this book, you are probably a rule-breaker and a gambler! And because I wrote it, well, I probably am too!

In fact, I'm one of the world's worst rule-breakers. I'm certainly not a team player. And I'm pretty rebellious – it is hard for me to stick by my own rules.

Share going down? Bah! Stops are for other people, the egotistical side of me says. Oh no they aren't, says my shark or Vulcan side: get out now you idiot!

I'm always trying to become more like a Vulcan and less like an idiot. I hope this book helps you in the same struggle. (Not that I'm calling you an idiot... er, you know what I meant!)

Always remember:

- treat trading as a business: seek to preserve your capital, make plans, be ruthless

- understand your emotions and eliminate their impact on your trading

- be aware of outside influences and be careful about how they affect your trading.

If you understand how important discipline is, you *can* change from failure to success.

It's not for everyone. I've met some people who just aren't suited to it. It's not a reflection on your character so don't feel bad about it. It's just one of those things. If you find you have tried for ages but can't make any money out of trading, or continue to make losses, then you have to stop.

Admitting failure is a successful thing to do. It means you can move on with your life and spend time doing other things. What you don't want to do is to end up like the people in some of the stories in this book who lost fortunes.

Even as the writer of this book I sometimes struggle with trading and when I fall into undisciplined behaviour I have to deal with it by giving myself a strict talking to. Having a tiny gambling account just for fun on the side does help!

I don't wish you all the best of luck, indeed no luck at all. I should say, I wish you all the best of *discipline*. And I hope you make it. But if you don't – there are plenty of other pleasures in life including one I have lined up for right now, now that I've finished this.

Right, where is the Mrs?

The shark rulebook

1. Always treat trading as a business.

2. Never attempt a trade when your brain is impaired by anything bad that is happening in your life.

3. Every trade must have an exit plan.

4. Every trade must have an idea of time scale.

5. Do not let any emotions cloud your judgement.

6. Weigh up negatives before ever pressing buy.

7. Ensure a trade has everything going for it.

8. Do not trade when feeling bored or fed up.

9. Never chase volatile markets.

10. In down markets, think about offsetting losses in your portfolio with a short on indices. (Be careful with indices at any other time, though!)

11. Do not listen to others on social media.

12. Beware everything you read or that is broadcast to you.

13. Never smear jam on your keyboard.

(After giving you these rules, well, of course, you are going to break some – but if you do break them, break them like a Vulcan: logically!)

The Quiz

Now you've read the book, find out whether you are a shark, someone on the way to that status, or a trader who's just going to end up sleeping with the fishes...

1. The market is plunging down. There seems no reason for this. What do you do?

a – Put on a short, that should help by making some money on the downside.

b – Put on a long, the market will recover and I can buy cheap stuff now.

c – Topslice some shares, do a short, see where the market goes next.

d – Look around the internet for news and figure out from that what to do next.

e – Buy, and buy more, it is sales time.

2. A share you bought has hit its stop-loss. Do you:

a – Buy some more and average up.

b – Sell it, or allow your automated stop you set up to be hit.

c – Sell half of it so if it goes back up you are still in.

d – Take the dog for a walk, hopefully when you are back it will be back up.

e – Stay with it for now, it will probably come back.

3. Your girlfriend dumped you last night. Do you:

a – Forget trading and get right onto Justdumpedneedsex.com?

b – Moan to your trading mates on Twitter?

c – Go to the pub for consolation drinks then trade in the afternoon?

d – Get trading to make loads – you'll show her.

e – Make sure you have stops on and leave trading alone today.

4. A great bloke on Twitter bought a share. Do you:

a – Follow him in, he's on a roll.

b – Short it.

c – Have a look at it from a negative viewpoint.

d – Make a note to research it.

e – Just buy it but stick a stop on.

5. The FTSE has gone down a lot. Do you:

a – Buy it, it's bound to go up now.

b – Short it, it'll probably go down more.

c – Keep buying and selling, see which way it goes.

d – Sell all your shares you've had enough.

e – Leave it well alone.

6. You researched a share – it looks amazing. Do you:

a – Get stuck in for a good amount.

b – Go back and check for negatives.

c – Check again, buy small with a tight stop.

d – Feel very excited about it and get a wad of it.

e – Buy it and tell all your trading mates on Twitter.

7. You nearly bought something a month ago and now it's a lot higher. Do you:

a – Swear at the screen and hope it goes down.

b – Short the bloody thing, make some on the downside.

c – Get stuck in, it owes me.

d – Research it as if you never saw it before.

e – Moan at yourself that you are crap at trading.

8. You have a share that has tanked 70%. Do you:

a – Just get rid of the bastard.

b – Average down and get more, you can still make a profit.

c – Keep it, no point selling it now.

d – Pump it on the bulletin boards try and get the price up.

e – Keep willing the **** to go up every day.

9. A friend recommends this great Forex signals service. Do you:

a – Get yourself a new friend.

b – Give it a go, Forex is all about signals.

c – Research it, the service is making loads, buy it.

d – Go to a seminar on how to trade Forex.

e – Try and find someone that made money on it over a year.

10. Your spread betting profits are booming. Do you:

a – Bank profits and use that to leverage up more.

b – Boast to everyone how amazing you are.

c – Start your own tipping service.

d – Feel overjoyed and buy even more risky shares.

e – Keep banking profits and put some in the actual bank.

Answers

1 – a o b o c 5 d 2 e o

2 – a o b 5 c 1 d o e o

3 – a 1 b 1 c o d o e 5

4 – a o b o c 5 d 4 e 1

5 – a o b 1 c 5 d o e o

6 – a o b 4 c 5 d o e o

7 – a o b o c o d 5 e 1

8 – a 5 b o c o d o e o

9 – a 3 b o c o d o e 5

10 – a 1 b o c o d o e 5

45+

You *are* a shark. Congratulations, go forth and trade. The oceans are yours.

31–44

Nearly a shark but not there yet. You have some work to do on your emotions before putting on another trade.

21–30

Not close to shark status – but there's a little promise there. Do lots more reading but definitely stop trading till you treat it like a business.

20 and under

Oh dear, it looks like you've just been shot by a harpoon. I suppose you could salvage something by trying to get 50p from selling this book on eBay.

Offers

Seminars

If you'd like to spend a day with Robbie and trade live markets at one of his seminars email **robbiethetrader@aol.com** for details. The seminars are designed for beginners and improvers. Learn how to research and time trades with live level 2 learning, as well as how to scan for trades.

Stockopedia

Stockopedia is *the* Vulcan trading website – it has all the cold logical facts and figures you need to trade well, with lots of share screens, including one based on my book *The Naked Trader*. There are also guru screens based on market legends like Warren Buffett. For £50 off and a free trial, go to: **www.stockopedia.com/nakedtrader**

My site

www.nakedtrader.co.uk features my fortnightly diary with my trades and views on the world. Check it out!

Index

THANKS
FOR READING!

Our readers mean everything to us at Harriman House. As a special thank-you for buying this book let us help you save as much as possible on your next read:

If you've never ordered from us before, get £5 off your first order at **harriman-house.com** with this code: `shrk51`

Already a customer? Get £5 off an order of £25 or more with this code: `shrk55`

Get 7 days' FREE access to hundreds of our books at **volow.co** – simply head over and sign up.

Thanks again!
from the team at

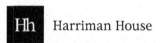

CPSIA information can be obtained
at www.ICGtesting.com
Printed in the USA
BVOW06s0913161116

468027BV00004B/90/P

9 780857 195425